The Afterlife of Property

DOMESTIC SECURITY

AND THE VICTORIAN NOVEL

✳

JEFF NUNOKAWA

PRINCETON UNIVERSITY PRESS

PRINCETON, NEW JERSEY

Library of Congress Cataloging-in-Publication Data
Nunokawa, Jeff, 1958–
The afterlife of property : domestic security and
the Victorian novel / Jeff Nunokawa.
p.   cm.
Includes bibliographical references (p.) and index.
ISBN 0-691-03320-X (alk. paper)
1. English fiction—19th century—History and criticism.
2. Domestic fiction, English—History and criticism.
3. Domestic relations in literature.   4. Homosexuality in
literature.   5. Property in literature.   6. Marriage in literature.
7. Women in literature.   8. Sex in literature.   I. Title.
PR878.D65N86   1994   828′.8—dc20   93-30912 CIP

This book has been composed in Adobe Galliard typeface

Princeton University Press books are printed on
acid-free paper and meet the guidelines for permanence
and durability of the Committee on Production Guidelines for
Book Longevity of the Council on Library Resources

Printed in the United States of America

1   3   5   7   9   10   8   6   4   2

❊ *Contents* ❊

✳ *Acknowledgments* ✳

I HAVE LOOKED FORWARD for a long time to the moment when I would be able to thank the friends, teachers, colleagues, and acquaintances who have made this book possible. Many must be unaware of the help they supplied—sometimes no more than a perspicacious suggestion, sometimes no less than a way of life. They have provoked my best efforts and consoled me when I found it impossible to sustain them. Among these I thank first those who have read versions of the manuscript and offered advice and encouragement that made it possible for me to complete it: Amanda Anderson, Laura Brown, Bob Brown, Judith Butler, Cynthia Chase, Walter Cohen, Jonathan Culler, Ann Cvetkovich, Larry Danson, Maria DiBattista, Lynn Enterline, Billy Flesch, Judith Frank, John Guillory, Lanny Hammer, Rosemary Kegl, Tom Keenan, Uli Knoepflmacher, Deborah Nord, Adela Pinch, Jim Richardson, Lora Romero, Eve Kosofsky Sedgwick, Mark Seltzer, Elaine Showalter, Margery Sokoloff, Jennifer Wicke, and an anonymous reader at Princeton University Press.

For help harder to name, I thank Alice Augenti, Phil Barish, Peter Brown, Leslie Brisman, Jill Campbell, Christina Crosby, Richard Elovich, Judy Foster, Diana Fuss, Richard Halpern, Beth Harrison, Phil Harper, Albert O. Hirschman, Walter Hughes, Molly Iuerelli, Haunani Lemn, Jack Levinson, Ann Lewis, Dave Lewis, Wellington Love, Loring McAlpin, Martin McElhiney, Wednesday T. Martin, Michael Meister, Carl Millholland, Wendy Millholland, David Miller, Dick Moran, John Murphy, Jill Nunokawa, Joyce Nunokawa, Scott Nunokawa, Walter Nunokawa, Lee Putnam, Laura Quinney, Gabriel Ramirez, Marcia Rosh, Adam Rolston, Andrew Ross, Joan Scott, Jim Siegel, Doreen Simpson, Sasha Torres, Tony Vidler, Sharon Willis, and Daniel Wolfe.

The Afterlife of Property

✳

Introduction

Think how terrible the fascination of money is! . . . I have
money always in my thoughts and my desires; and the whole life
I place before myself is money, money, money, and what money
can make of life!
(*Bella Wilfer, in* Our Mutual Friend)

TRANSFORMATIONS OF CAPITAL

THIS BOOK begins with the fears entertained in and beyond the Victorian novel about the powers of the commodity as they are embodied in four representative works written during the quarter-century Eric Hobsbawm calls the age of capital:[1] *Little Dorrit* (1855), *Dombey and Son* (1848), *Daniel Deronda* (1876), and *Silas Marner* (1861). As Bella Wilfer knows, the terrible fascination of money is inseparable from the fascination of its conquests. Plots such as those I will survey here to restrict the grasp of the commodity are plots to limit the expansiveness that is the most common source of anxiety about it.[2] For capitalism's discontents, the scandal of an economy characterized by the comprehensive grasp of the commodity form is the well-known story of its further spread, what Hobsbawm calls "the major theme" (xi–xii) of the third quarter of the nineteenth century, a theme whose modern and postmodern variations have resonated no less consequentially in the years since.

Such expansion has never been thought to confine itself to conquests at home or abroad of new outposts for trade or new sources of labor; more intimate infiltrations have always been noticed at work alongside capitalism's grander annexations; generations of its critics have traced its marks in the innermost recesses and resources of the cultures whose economy it comprehends; generations of capitalism's critics have witnessed it colonize all sorts of values defined by their difference from what can be bought and sold, transforming, Midas-like, everything it touches into tools or mirrors of its own image.

Ever renovated, this crisis of capital is nothing new: if the middle of the nineteenth century crowns the age that historians of capitalism identify as the period of its classic style and highest hopes,[3] the age of capital was thick with detractors, alarmed that market values had managed to engross everything under the sun; the nation of shopkeepers was loud with voices prosecuting the by-now familiar charge that the luster of commodities had eclipsed all other visions of value: "All the Truth of this Universe is uncertain; only the profit and loss of it . . . remain very visible to the practical man."[4]

However else we may have broken from the Victorian frame of mind, its outlines remain visible in our apprehension, traumatized or routine, that the commodity form, like a triumphal army or a thief in the night, has entranced regions of the psyche, precincts of culture and forms of labor whose worth had been measured by their distance from market value. Victorian prophets against the empire of the cash nexus have readied us to regard the "deity" Bulwer-Lytton declared "the mightiest of all,"[5] a strange god, come to rule where he doesn't belong; their suspicions persist in our inclination to remark the spread of market values as a brand of invasion; their voluble impeachments can be heard even now in the sound of everyday attitudes of annoyance and anxiety about the "commodification of everything."[6]

They reverberate as well through a tradition of cultural criticism inaugurated by Marx's meditations on the ideological aspects of capitalism, a tradition that has distinguished itself exposing the endless adumbrations of the commodity form beyond the commonly recognized borders of the marketplace, measuring its refractions through the prisms of reification all across the social horizon, discerning its comprehension, day and night, of the entire ensemble of social practices.[7]

But our sense of the commodity's invasiveness may owe its largest debt neither to the eloquences of social prophecy, no matter how urgent, nor to the elaborations of social theory, no matter how perspicacious, but rather to the Victorian novel and its narrative heirs; for here, the diffuse, diffusive, subject of commodification comes home. The nineteenth-century novel never ceases remarking the reach of market forces into the parlors, bedrooms, and closets of a domestic realm that thus never ceases to fail in its mission to shelter its inhabitants from the clash of these armies. More often than not, this most influential of domestic monitors observes the saving distance between home and marketplace only in its breach. The novel's celebration of domesticity as a sanctuary from the vicissitudes of the cash nexus is everywhere spoiled; everywhere the shades of the countinghouse fall upon the home.

"How changed the house is, though! The front is patched over with bills, setting forth the particulars of the furniture in staring capitals."[8] The bankruptcy auctions that erupt like occasional earthquakes upon the domestic landscape of the Victorian novel only begin to tell how the household goes the way of all capital even within—perhaps especially within—the literary form most interested in promoting the home as the place where the man busy all day getting and spending might finally have some peace. These spectacular household failures serve notice of a ubiquitous insecurity; the buyers who "swarm the halls" and "invade the upper apartments, pinching the bed-curtains, poking into the feathers," make examples of the domestic establishments they dissolve: these bleak houses remind all who see them that the forces of the market know where everybody lives.

The auctioneer's housebreaking works to realize the pervasive condition of commodification that manages to hold all homes under constant threat: whenever household goods are put up for sale, we have reason to recall that they always can be. While such terroristic extensions of the market's long arm into the domestic realm are rare, they, like the arrival there of death—and the police—are frequent enough to remind everyone that they are always ready, always ready because the shape of the commodity, like the sentence of mortality and the watch of the law, comprehends all that dwells in the vanity fair described but hardly contained by the Victorian novel: "Down comes the hammer like fate, and we move on to the next lot" (201).

And the furniture is the least of it: the traumatic spectacle of "mattresses," "spotless linen," and "rich and complete set[s] of family plate" (201) on the block pales before the luster of another, far richer household good never far from the auctioneer's hammer. In the Victorian novel, the shock of commodification, whose broad waves leave no home untouched, conducts its greatest charge in the domestic scandal Barbara Bodichon calls a "disgusting exhibition," "often seen in our country": "a man . . . going through the farce of a sale, and exhibiting his wife with a halter round her neck."[9]

The conviction that the grasp of the market exceeds its proper reach when it traffics in women is upheld by a cultural consensus busy a century later recycling Victorian condemnations of prostitution and the marriage market.[10] And just as it did in the nineteenth century, this prohibition expresses itself to greatest effect now in the fanfare that surrounds its defeat, in the transgressive allure that attends its violation, in, for example, the now routine thrill of illicitness incited by the spectacle of human commodities who, frankly owning themselves as such, know how to turn the profit to themselves.

If women's designs to sell themselves have acquired an affirmative charge, this is because they are thus at least no longer sold by others; modern materializations, blond or platinum, of Becky Sharp's ambitions reverse the subjection of women as eminent Victorians like Mill, Dickens, and Eliot tell it; the charisma that enwraps those who know that diamonds are a girl's best friend recalls, even while inverting, the "self-abasement, and the burning indignation" of more than "a hundred women"; the "self-abasement, and the burning indignation" that *Dombey and Son* phrases as the feelings of living property: "There is no slave in a market . . . so shown and offered and examined and paraded as I have been . . . hawked and vended here and there, until the last grain of self-respect is dead within me."[11]

Such spectacles dismantle the boundary with which several centuries of discursive formation have sought to separate woman's estate from the anxiety of the marketplace.[12] Anyone who has ever read a Victorian novel or lived on the family plan it helped devise has felt the force of its conviction that a man's home is his castle, a shelter from the mean streets of the cash nexus, and that a woman—a wife, a mother, a daughter—oversees this estate. And a woman's work is never done: the angel of the house is the spirit of this domain not only because she supervises it, but also because she constitutes it.[13]

Essence and ornament of a domestic sphere defined by its distance from the marketplace, the angel of the house is a kind of value that transcends the commodity form. According to the ecstatic evaluations championed by the likes of Coventry Patmore, no price can be put on the woman whose husband holds her dear: "Her graces make him rich, and ask / No guerdon" ("The Angel in the House"). Attempts to measure the monetary worth of her crystal virtues only confirm what a colder economist of married love calls her "incalculable value."[14]

Like the slave auction with which it is persistently linked, the marriage market is often less a scandal of possession than a scandal for possession. "The evil of slavery," Walter Benn Michaels observes in a revisionist parsing of abolitionist sentiment, "lies . . . not in its reversion to a barbaric paternalism but in its uncanny way of epitomizing . . . market society." If the peculiar institution is common after all, if human property embodies rather than predates or transcends the commodity form, then slaves are as risky a business as "Shares" or savings and loans. As

Michaels reads her, the crisis of slavery for Harriet Beecher Stowe is the "insecurity" that is "the inevitable fate of property in a free market,"[15] a fate that spells out not only the possible, but the inevitable loss of property in the nineteenth-century imagination that I will take up here.

A similar distress afflicts the human goods housed by the home department (*DS*) of the Victorian novel: trauma ensues there when wives are called commodities, not because they are thus cast as property, but rather because such property is thus cast among the uncertainties of the marketplace. Trouble arises when women are cast as such property in the Victorian novel less because the proprietor's grasp goes too far when it reaches her than because that grasp is always loosened when the shadow of the commodity falls upon the object that it holds. Undoing the boundary between the woman a man loves and the property he owns, the mercenary marriage dissolves the distinction between a species of property that is normally, or at least normatively, secure and one that is bound to be lost.[16]

Nothing could hurt more in the Victorian novel, where to have property is to settle in life and to lose it a taste of death, a scandal, a terror, a tragedy in which all others gather, a catastrophe where the various meanings of ruin convene, a calamity that causes everything in and out of sight to tremble:

> "The fact is," said Mr. Brogley, "there's a little payment on a bond debt—three hundred and seventy odd, over due: and I'm in possession."
>
> "In possession!" cried Walter, looking round the shop.
>
> "Ah!" said Mr. Brogley. . . . "It's an execution. . . ."
>
> . . . Everything seemed altered as [Walter] ran along the streets. . . . Houses and shops were different from what they used to be, and bore Mr. Brogley's warrant on their fronts in large characters. The broker seemed to have got hold of the very churches. . . . Even the sky itself was changed, and had an execution in it plainly. (*DS* 177–78)

Injuries like this are sometimes the consequence of blunder or treachery; the heart-stopping failure that leaves Brogley in possession results, for example, from the shopkeeper's inability to keep up with changes in consumer demand. The Victorian novel is filled with stolen and squandered fortunes, large and small, with thefts conducted in the dead of night or during business hours, with follies less criminal but no less culpable.

But these are only part of the story. According to the calculations I will audit in *Little Dorrit*, *Dombey and Son*, and *Daniel Deronda*, it's not just that property fit to circulate in the market might be parted from its owner, it must be. In the texts I will consider in the chapters that follow, such grave losses result less from accident or avarice than from laws of the marketplace situated beyond the province of human error. Taking to heart headlines announcing the risks of the marketplace, headlines no less sensational in the middle of the nineteenth century than they are now—"Hectic Booms Alternate with Financial Panics"; "Business Magnate and . . . Investor . . . Haunted by Specters of Bankruptcy"[17]—the economic imagination I will audit locates the origin of such losses in the nature of the market and of marketable property rather than in the will or weakness of individuals.

Moreover, while the forces of alienation I will investigate here comprehend the market and marketable property, they are not confined to these things. It's not only money, and what can be converted into money, that must be relinquished according to the assessments I will investigate, but also "forms of capital" that dwell beyond the cash nexus; it's not only the market that demands the loss of property, but also "modes of circulation" located outside its bounds.[18]

In *Little Dorrit*, the loss of property is compelled by the rule of exchange that regulates the transfer of a broad range of capital. When the mother of a guilt-ridden heir observes that he regards the hard-got family fortune as so much "plunder"[19] that must be renounced, she describes more than filial ingratitude; she describes the general economy of the novel, an economy that ensures that anything taken will be taken away. While the law of exchange is less explicit here than it is where what is acquired has a price tag, it is no less compelling: The circle of gain and loss that makes any acquisition a kind of debt in *Little Dorrit* is like the exotic cultures where Western anthropologists find in primitive or archaic circuits of giving and getting the logic of exchange hard at work far away from the regions of the commodity form.[20]

When property is cast as either economic or symbolic capital in *Dombey and Son*, as either "money" (77) or the "capital of the House's name," it is a form of public address that corrodes the boundaries of exclusivity that define private property generally, and especially in this novel. Whether it is the firm that the haughty financier can share only with the son who is no more than his own reflection or his "sense of property" in that son, a sense destroyed by the thought that anyone else may share him, possession, in *Dombey and Son*, is "exclusion itself"

8

(*DS* 159). Moreover, in an agoraphobic amplification of the exclusivity of private property, *Dombey and Son* extends its borders to reserve for the owner even the knowledge of what is owned. If, according to the idea of property with which we are most familiar, to own is to own alone, to own alone in *Dombey and Son* is to own in secret, and, correlatively, to publicize property is to lose it.

A sense of the privacy of property this refined is too delicate to withstand the exhibitionism of capital, whose sometimes garish but always showy signs are available to anyone who can see, hear, or read. An expressiveness we are inclined to read as thoroughly postmodern, to attach to a society of spectacle or a landscape of simulacrum, was no less active by the middle of the nineteenth century. The capital we cannot help but get in our eyes now is no less spectacular in *Dombey and Son*, where "money makes us powerful and glorious in the eyes of all men" (152–3); where "gold and silver" are "demonstrations" (584), where the noise of the streets consists of "commodities . . . addressed to the general public" (237), where the "capital of the House's name" is ready for the taking by all who can read Dombey and Son, or *Dombey and Son*.

The urge toward alienation that *Dombey and Son* ascribes to capital *Daniel Deronda* attributes to the condition of possessing it: ownership in *Daniel Deronda* is an intermediate stage rather than a stable state, a phase of a "drama" sometimes so quick that only a "moment hand" can measure its length, a transitional administration whose sole function is to prepare its own passing. Here the power to bestow[21] that defines the ownership of capital is the end of an irresistible trajectory;[22] here the power to bestow is transformed into the compulsion to do so: ownership of capital in *Daniel Deronda* is driven inexorably to its conclusion. Like the drive toward death or the principle of narrative with which ownership is affiliated in Eliot's novel, possession is the work of its own termination.

A rule of exchange that, accepting no substitutions, exacts the loss of anything acquired, a sense of property's privacy that is abrogated by capital's inherent exhibitionism, a definition of capital ownership that characterizes it as the work of its own cancellation: such rules ensure that the alienability which is the signature condition of capital—both what enables it, as well as its dominant aspect—never rests. Like a heat-seeking missile or the teleological subject of History or Therapy, capital never fails to realize its potential.

DOMESTIC ECONOMIES

When these various forms of capital and their "corresponding modes of circulation" comprehend a man's wife, they ruin a last resort for the secure property endlessly sought but seldom found in the Victorian novel. What a man, at the end of a hard day's unprofitable work or a long novel of financial disaster, "lock[s] in his arms" and "h[o]ld[s] to his heart" is a brand of property supposed immune from loss. On the verge of their wedding, such property typically declares its own value to the man who claims it: "Never to part, my dearest . . . never any more, until the last! . . . I am yours, anywhere, everywhere!"[23]

The effect of vows like this, shocking in their very familiarity, extends beyond the novel: Victorian arraignments of marriage as the modern form of woman's subjection, as well as Victorian celebrations of it as the form of her fulfillment, recognized a man's possession of his wife as safe estate. It was her status as such during the Victorian era that mitigated the habitual comparison of the condition of wives to that of the nineteenth century's most infamous instance of human property.[24] Even where its kinship to this state remains unpronounced, slavery, according to some of its most influential discontents, defines the deep structure of women's position in Victorian England. John Stuart Mill's compendium of women's subjection defines relations between men and women as an extension of those between master and slave; any disparity between these terms is the result of accidental attenuations that do nothing to alter their genetic intimacy. *The Subjection of Women* is crowded with comparisons between the house of married love and Uncle Tom's cabin, ("'Uncle Tom' under his first master had his own life in his 'cabin' . . . but it cannot be so with the wife"); between the legal and sexual subjugation of wives and slaves: "a female slave has (in Christian countries) an admitted right, and is considered under a moral obligation, to refuse to her master the last familiarity. Not so the wife"; "the wife is the actual bondservant of her husband: no less so, as far as the legal obligation goes, than slaves commonly so called." Sometimes the slavery of women is worse than that of "slaves commonly so called," sometimes better, but Mill, and several generations of English feminists with him, is everywhere dedicated to exposing the two as variations of the same property.[25]

But whatever the similarities between wives and slaves "commonly so called," they were generally distinguished not only by the color of their skin, but also by their character as property; for while slaves were at least typically assessed as goods that could circulate from owner to owner, wives were defined as virtually inalienable treasure.[26] What for another Victorian feminist is a rule whose violation is the last straw of women's subjection ("the belief that a man can rid himself of his wife by going through the farce of a sale"),[27] is for Mill, in an argument no less potent for its facetiousness, a rule whose enforcement deprives women of their only opportunity to alleviate it:

> Surely, if a woman is denied any lot in life but that of being the personal body-servant of a despot, and is dependent for everything upon the chance of finding one who may be disposed to make a favourite of her instead of merely a drudge, it is a very cruel aggravation of her fate that she should be allowed to try this chance only once. The natural sequel and corollary from this state of things would be, that since her all in life depends upon obtaining a good master, she should be allowed to change again and again until she finds one. (*Subjection of Women*, 33)

Mill argues that a woman should be able to retain the right at least to choose who owns her; Bodichon assumes that this prerogative would rest as a matter of course with the owner himself. But both affirm the exceptional status of this property; whether for better or worse, whether by a rule that makes her subjection permanent or by a rule that limits it, title to such estate cannot be readily transferred.

Woman's status as unportable property enriches our sense of the economic dimensions of the domestic sphere with which she is associated. Efforts to determine the economics of the domestic sphere have usually taken the form of impeaching the claim that it is removed from market practices and values; starting in the nineteenth century, feminist dissenters from the House of Ruskin have traditionally assessed domestic relations as a covert continuation of market exchange. Thus, Susan Kent reports, Victorian feminists employed "a commercial idiom" to expose the market realities that persist in the domestic sphere;[28] in *Three Guineas*, Virginia Woolf describes the work of middle- and upper-class women in and beyond the Victorian period as wages by another name;[29] more recent Marxist-feminist accounts have noticed how the removal of women from the ranks of wage earners during the nineteenth century worked to disguise rather than transcend the economic value of their labor.[30]

11

More recently still, feminist assessments of Victorian domestic ideology in and beyond the novel have exposed the cult of separate spheres
as a means of strengthening and stabilizing the market economy by
providing intermittent relief from their conflicts and contradictions.[31]
The home whose ideological dimensions Mary Poovey and Nancy Armstrong survey is a complex of money-laundering operations, a place
where the war of all against all, or the one between the classes, or the
split within the self, brought on by this economy is suspended or cured.
According to their various accounts, the domestic sphere, whose essence
is the love of a good woman, offers a vacation from the pressures of the
market economy, or translates the terms of its divisions and divisiveness
from the marketplace where they are invented and exacerbated into a
sphere of romance where they are resolved.[32] Under the sharp lens of
their scrutiny, a simple image of home as a haven in a heartless world
gives way to the more complex vision of a site for the imaginary resolution of antagonisms that the market economy starts and cannot solve.
The domestic devotions they examine assist the operations of the market
economy exactly as Victorians themselves thought a wife should: by fur-
nishing the place where the perturbations of the marketplace are put
to rest.

But the economic value of woman's estate surpasses the hidden—if
by now familiar—extension of the market economy into the domestic
realm; it surpasses the support that the domestic realm delivers to the
market economy in its very difference from the market economy; it surpasses even the "forms of capital" and their "corresponding modes of
circulation" different from but analogous to those of the marketplace.
It entertains as well a prospect of secure property available to the bourgeois male, a prospect of property that transcends all tokens and avenues
of circulation.

To appreciate fully the economic value of the woman that a man has
by the end of a Victorian novel requires a sense of the economic expanded not only beyond the bounds of the marketplace, but beyond
even the sites of circulation that are cast outside it. What one reader
condemns as a "mixing of . . . economic advantages into relations which
ought to be based on affection and human need" in the "mercenary
marriage" advertised in the Victorian novel is a confusion not of the economic and noneconomic, or even a sphere of exchange commonly recognized as such, with a sphere where exchange takes place less visibly,
but rather of the zone of circulation and the zone of possession.[33] The

difference between the angel of the house and the prostitute of the parlor or the streets is the difference between a species of property thought
safe from one that never can be, the difference between forms and forces
that expand indefinitely beyond the arena of the commodity and a kind
of estate exempted from all its vicissitudes.

NOVEL PROPERTY

But, as we have already seen in the spectacle of the marriage market, the
distance between domestic securities and the vicissitudes of capital circulation cannot be saved. With the regularity of the downward turn
charted by epic hero and business cycle, the angel of the house is discharged from her situation as safe estate and subject to the restless fate
of capital: the property celebrated for its exceptional security meets the
fate of all that circulates. In *Little Dorrit*, for example, women are in-
ducted into the cycle of debt that liquidates property generally; in *Dombey and Son*, women, no less than money or the house's name, are cast
as forms of capital subject to the alienating effects of publicity. But even
as Dickens and Eliot measure the exposure of women's estate to the
tides of circulation, they labor all the while to prepare new grounds
where renovations of this estate will be safe from its strong currents.
Securities lost on the tides of circulation gain firmer ground in a new
domesticity, passed over by the forces that ruin the first.

The final return home plotted by novels like *Little Dorrit*, *Dombey
and Son*, and *Daniel Deronda* finds that place of peace less restored than
reformed. Like the fortunes of capitalism that a Protestant ethic reads as
the talent of the spirit, the feminine treasure that eludes the vicissitudes
of capital finds her home among the intangible figments of the heart and
mind rather than the items of the object world. What can't be held *to* the
heart for long can be held *in* it forever: property that can't be kept up in
the external world is sustained instead in the figure of a woman whose
dimensions are defined less by the material shapes of house or body than
by a lover's fond thoughts or sorrowful memory. Correlatively, the limits that the demands of circulation impose on the power of ownership
are circumvented when its field of operation is not a physical object, but
rather the incessant fantasies of "living property."

And the imaginations of women who evade the current of circulation
merge with the imagination of the novel that contains them. We have

13

already begun to observe the opposite: the novel's tendency to identify capital with aspects of its own form. "The capital of the House's name" merges with the title of the text that contains it; capital's drive toward alienation takes shape as a narrative aim to achieve its end in *Daniel Deronda*. But if capital assumes the forms of the novel, so does the property that eludes it: the imagined figures diverted from the certain loss that defines capital dwell in a reformed domesticity, a new interiority enfolded within the pages of the novel, or within the experience of reading it. When property is released from the mortal coils of capital in the fiction I will scrutinize here, it does so *as* fiction, as a rhetorical afterlife that arises from the ashes of exchange, as a fragment of literary fantasy that men can keep to themselves, and as a narrative whose always anticipated conclusion never comes.

The woman that Arthur Clennam holds by the end of the novel consists of a fictional treasure that is only allegorically connected to a previous acquisition and thus exempt from the rule of exchange that requires the loss of anything gained. Little Dorrit is safe property for the man who marries her because this elegiac estate is as distant from the circuit of exchange as an echo is from its origin or a sign is from its referent. A woman whom a man can hold in secret and thus hold securely in *Dombey and Son* comes from the pages of a ballad book or from a memory of the *Arabian Nights*, scraps of text that a man can entertain within the privacy of his own mind. In *Daniel Deronda*, the version of proprietorial prerogative constrained by the lockstep teleology of capital ownership gives way to a wife's endless fantasies of her husband's power, fantasies that conclude always before the realization, and thus the exhaustion, of his mastery: Gwendolen Grandcourt's "fancy" ends, or fails to end, with her husband's hand "cling[ing] round her neck and *threaten[ing]* to throttle her" (my emphasis).[34] Through these fantasies, the husband's power achieves an ongoingness that distinguishes it from the doomed regime of proprietorial prerogative that defines the ownership of capital; it achieves an ongoingness that Roland Barthes congratulates as the pensiveness of the classic text: "The classic text is pensive: replete with meaning . . . it still seems to be keeping in reserve some ultimate meaning . . . which is the theatrical sign of the implicit."[35]

These novel properties augment the ensemble of relations between economics and the house of fiction audited by several generations of literary criticism. If the work of fiction is a reflection, evasion, or imaginary resolution of a discrete economy, it is also an economic form itself.[36] The woman in whom the interests of property are finally secured is the subject or object of a rhetorical effect, which manages to sustain the saving distance from the sphere of circulation that real estate, whether defined by the walls of a house or the body of its star occupant, cannot.

FOREIGN RELATIONS: SEX, RACE, AND THE ANGEL OF THE HOUSE

But the Victorian novel relies on more than its own resources to establish secure estate. If it turns inward, to the forms of fiction itself, to find material for such property, it turns to more exotic regions to underwrite the difference of such property from the sphere of circulation. The distance that shelters domestic treasure from the tides of circulation that would render her insecure is supported by her distance from various foreign bodies. Transcending the sphere of circulation involves methods of containment that associate the operations of capital with scapegoats culled from catalogs of foreign races and illicit sexualities available in the nineteenth century. By attaching capital to figures of exotic and doomed races, or particular identities and intensities of sexual desire slated for extinction, the Victorian novel arranges the death or abjection of circulation, and thus the endless life of property beyond it.

In *Dombey and Son*, capital is identified with the "oriental" and thus subject to the bodily decay that the novel casts as the fate of the "Oriental" generally. According to a construction of the non-Western that Dickens's novel engages, the Oriental is confined to the body and thus subject to the limitations of the flesh. By fastening capital to this body, *Dombey and Son* imposes mortal limits on what is otherwise an endless metaphysical life—the one described by the financier's elation at the beginning of the novel:

> A.D. had no concern with anno Domini, but stood for anno Dombei—and Son.
>
> He had risen, as his father had before him, in the course of life and death, from Son to Dombey, and for nearly twenty years had been the sole representative of the Firm. (50)

Dombey's calculations give the local color of character to a more general conviction about the abstractness of the commodity form: "Not an

atom of matter enters into the objectivity of commodities as values,"
Marx declares in a famous meditation on the sublime object of capitalism. "In this it is the direct opposite of the coarsely sensuous objectivity
of commodities as physical bodies."[37] Whether it is the house's name or
the commodity form, capital emits no odor of the body:

> There, in the market-place and in shop windows, things stand still.
> They are under the spell of one activity only; to change owners. They
> stand there waiting to be sold. While they are there for exchange they
> are there not for use. A commodity marked out at a definite price, for
> instance, is looked upon as being frozen to absolute immutability
> throughout the time during which its price remains unaltered. And the
> spell does not only bind the doings of man. Even nature herself is sup-
> posed to abstain from any ravages in the body of this commodity and to
> hold her breath, as it were, for the sake of this social business of man.
> Evidently, even the aspect of non-human nature is affected by the ban-
> ishment of use from the sphere of exchange.[38]

This metaphysical spell is broken when capital is mixed with the body of
the Orient: When capital is Orientalized, it is incarnated and thus subject to the mortal fate that it otherwise evades. And from its corpse rises
the figure of a woman, white as a ghost, whose endearments a man can
keep to himself.[39]

What is confined to an Oriental body in *Dombey and Son* is elsewhere
in the Victorian novel contained within the borders of particular versions of erotic desire. In *The Passions and the Interests*, Albert O. Hirschman describes the conviction prevalent during the seventeenth and eighteenth centuries that "one set of passions . . . greed, avarice, or love of
lucre could be usefully employed to oppose and bridle such other passions as ambition, lust for power, or sexual lust."[40] At the conclusion of
his book, Hirschman regretfully reports the cessation of hostilities—
even the dismantling of the difference—between economic and non-
economic desires. In *The Wealth of Nations*, Adam Smith draws up an
armistice between these warring parties, whose terms Hirschman reads
as the unconditional surrender of the passions to the interests:

> In [Smith's] most important and influential work . . . [t]here seems to
> be no place . . . for the richer concept of human nature in which men
> are driven by, and often torn between, diverse passions of which "ava-
> rice" was only one. . . . Smith . . . takes the final reductionist step of
> turning two into one . . . the noneconomic drives, powerful as they are,

are all made to feed into the economic ones and do nothing but rein-
force them, being thus deprived of their erstwhile independent existence. (108–9)

But if the dissolution of differences between the passions and the interests subordinates sexual desires to the exigencies of capitalism, the
expanded economy that results is now marked by the passions that they
have absorbed, erotic dimensionalities that only the flattening lens of
the drabbest economism would fail to notice:

> Hideous solidity was the characteristic of the Podsnap plate. Everything
> was made to look as heavy as it could, and to take up as much room as
> possible. Everything said boastfully, "Here you have as much of me in
> my ugliness as if I were only lead; but I am so many ounces of pre-
> cious metal worth so much an ounce; wouldn't you love to melt me
> down?"[41]

The taunt that emanates from this misshapen form in *Our Mutual
Friend* resembles one we are likely to associate with a body more beautiful: like the object of erotic obsession who knows full well its own irre-
sistibility, the commodity swaggers with the confidence that the offer it
makes cannot be refused.

But if the desire for the commodity resembles an undeniable sexual
attraction, it is unlike any that accords with our own Balkanized erotic
sensibilities. The passion for money transcends any local distinctions of
desire, such as that which distinguishes a subject who wants her own
gender from a subject who wants the other. While the appeal of an erotic
object is confined to a particular sector of desire, the urge to exchange
is assumed to be universal.

When the abstract appeal of the commodity form is conjoined with
the attractions of the erotic, the universality of the former sometimes
works to cancel the limitations imposed on the latter—as with models
familiar from any *Vanity Fair* whose moneyed allure transcends the particularities of sexual taste. But sometimes the power of capital shrinks to
the confines of particular sexualities. Thus, for example, in *Little Dorrit*
the hazards of circulation are at times concentrated in the "perversity"
of an odd woman, a perversity that culminates in her desire for a girl like
herself; in *Dombey and Son*, capital is leagued with a promiscuous sexuality that shares its destabilizing exhibitionism. Such sexualities, and with
them the vicissitudes of circulation to which they are attached, are made
to disappear through the offices of a heterosexual bias virtually indistin-

guishable from the generic outline of the Victorian plot, a bias that does not rest until it has finished preparing the house where a man can keep the woman he loves in peace.

But the threat of perversity is not neatly aligned with the forces of circulation in the Victorian novel; it is just as often leagued with efforts to evade them. In *Silas Marner* the specter of perversity gathers not only around the push and shove of capital circulation, but also around efforts to avoid it; here a flight from the sphere of circulation introduces rather than expunges a sexual threat. The gold that the miser seeks to remove from circulation is the object and agent of a sexual perversity that threatens a regime of propriety rather than the security of property.

Thus *Silas Marner* stands at the outer boundary of this book. *The Afterlife of Property* is concerned primarily with the economic imagination of the Victorian novel and with the ways that the Victorian novel inducts various figures of gender, rhetoric, race, and sexuality in the service of this imagination. In *Silas Marner*, we confront an anxiety that extends past the prospect of economic ruin, and a happy ending whose securities extend past its avoidance. If Dickens and Eliot describe an aversion to the instability of capital and a dream of possession that transcends it, they describe other forms and forces as well. Lurking within and beyond the interests of the economy are threats and pleasures that, no less than property and its enemies, are as much our own as they are the Victorians' who prepared them for us, and us for them.

Domestic Securities: *Little Dorrit* and the Fictions of Property

1

The first person who, having fenced off a plot of ground, took it into his head to say *this is mine* and found people simple enough to believe him, was the true founder of civil society. What crimes, wars, murders, what miseries and horrors would the human race have been spared by someone who, uprooting the stakes or filling in the ditch, had shouted to his fellow men: Beware of listening to this impostor; you are lost if you forget that the fruits belong to all and the earth to no one.[1]

Rousseau's famous story of the origin of ownership is actually two stories: If the formation of property brings about the maladies mentioned in this passage, property is in turn invented by an act of acquisition—the founder of civil society must first claim a plot of land in order to make it his. While Rousseau asserts that the founder of civil society engages in an act of theft when he appropriates something that previously did not belong to him, since "the fruits belong to all and the earth to no one," the liberal conception of property that R. H. Tawney calls "the Traditional Doctrine" regards possession as legitimate *only* when it results from such appropriation:

Whatever may have been the historical process by which [it has] been established and recognized, the *rationale* of private property traditional in England is that which sees in it either the results of the personal labour of its owner, or—what is in effect the same thing—the security that each man will reap what he has sown. Locke argued that a man necessarily and legitimately becomes the owner of "whatsoever he removes out of the state that nature hath provided."[2]

The acquisition that invents property is a crime, according to Rousseau, while a similar act justifies the property that is its fruit for "the Traditional Doctrine," but in either case, ownership is inaugurated by an act of appropriation. Both the founder of civil society and Locke's laborer own what they own by taking something that was not theirs before. The influence of the claim expressed in these passages is reflected in our conception of acquisition and ownership as the terms of a tautology: to possess is to take possession.

In the prospect of inheritance, *Little Dorrit* envisions a conception of property that troubles our sense of an inevitable intimacy between ownership and appropriation. Arthur Clennam illustrates the novel's wishful idea of inheritance in his proleptic announcement to Amy Dorrit of her father's fortune: "He will be a rich man. He is a rich man. A great sum of money is waiting to be paid over to him as his inheritance; you are all henceforth very wealthy."[3] Clennam's confusion of William Dorrit's future enfranchisement ("He will be a rich man") with his present condition ("He is a rich man") cancels the work of *taking* possession: Dorrit's inheritance is already his, property that waits to be discovered rather than appropriated. When he discloses the news of the legacy to William Dorrit himself, Clennam's proleptic assessment again removes the work of acquisition from the scene of the heir's enfranchisement:

> "Take a little time to think. To think of the brightest and most fortunate accidents of life. We have all heard of great surprises of joy. They are not at an end, sir. They are rare, but not at an end. Tell me Mr. Dorrit, what surprise would be the most unlooked for and the most acceptable to you . . ." He looked stedfastly at Clennam, and so looking at him, seemed to change into a very old haggard man. The sun was bright upon the wall beyond the window and on the spikes at top. He slowly stretched out the hand that had been upon his heart, and pointed at the wall. "It is down," said Clennam. "Gone! . . . And in its place," said Clennam slowly and distinctly, "are the means to possess and enjoy the utmost that they have so long shut out." (350)

Clennam begins by describing the moment of acquisition as a surprise or accident, as an event that evades perception because it occurs too quickly to be seen, or foreseen, but as he proceeds here, the disappearance of Dorrit's accession to ownership becomes more radical; the passage to possession disappears entirely. The wall that defines Dorrit's poverty will not come down, "it is down. . . . Gone!" Dorrit will not get treasure; he already has it: in place of the prison wall "are the means to possess and enjoy the utmost that they have so long shut out."

Only an immanent enfranchisement such as this is sheltered from the destabilizing rule of equivalent exchange that governs the economy of *Little Dorrit*, a rule that ensures that anything taken will be taken away. The novel literalizes and intensifies the iron law of equivalent exchange that governs the marketplace, generally, according to most accounts of it: in Dickens's novel, the acquisition of property does not merely require payment; such payment must consist of the very property acquired in the first place. Thus, when property is acquired in *Little Dorrit*, it must be relinquished.[4]

This rule condemns almost all property in the novel, since almost all property there, even inheritance, is marked by the signs of its acquisition. While Clennam's account of the Dorrits' legacy strains to cast it as the "rare but not extinct surprise" of unacquired allotment, inheritance is usually just another case of portable property. Little Dorrit's godfather cannot fashion a sufficiently secure inheritance to bequeath to her because he cannot circumvent the moment of its transmission and therefore cannot prevent its loss:

> He decided to will and bequeath his little property of savings to his godchild, and the point arose how could it be so "tied up" as that only she should have the benefit of it? His experience on the lock [at the Marshalsea] gave him such an acute perception of the enormous difficulty of "tying up" money with any approach to tightness, and contrariwise of the remarkable ease with which it got loose, that through a series of years he regularly propounded this knotty point to every new insolvent agent and other professional gentleman who passed in and out.
>
> "Supposing," he would say, stating the case with his key, on the professional gentleman's waistcoat, "supposing a man wanted to leave his property to a young female, and wanted to tie it up so that nobody else should ever be able to make a grab at it; how would you tie up that property?"
>
> "Settle it strictly on herself," the professional gentleman would complacently answer.
>
> "But look here," quoth the turnkey. "Supposing she had, say a brother, say a father, say a husband, who would be likely to make a grab at that property when she came into it—how about that?"
>
> "It would be settled on herself, and they would have no more legal claim on it than you," would be the professional answer.
>
> "Stop a bit," said the turnkey. "Supposing she was tender-hearted, and they came over her. Where's your law for tying it up then?"
>
> The deepest character whom the turnkey sounded, was unable to produce a law for tying such a knot as that. So the turnkey died intestate after all. (59)

The vague sense of guilt that inhabits all of Arthur Clennam's thoughts about his family fortune registers again the failure of inheritance to transcend the terms of gain and loss. "The shadow of a supposed act of injustice" (268) that darkens Clennam's inheritance throughout the novel is his suspicion that "in grasping at money . . . someone may have been grievously deceived, injured, ruined" (39). While the revelation that his stepmother stole Little Dorrit's annuity confirms Clennam's fear that his fortune includes money taken from someone else, it fails to account for the pervasiveness of his sense of guilt. It is not sufficent to explain why his apprehension, "so vague and formless [that] it might be the result of a reality widely remote from his idea of it," is enough to render him "ready at any moment to lay down all he had, and begin the world anew" (268), since the amount withheld from Little Dorrit would not have required Clennam to relinquish "all he had" in order to restore it to her.

Clennam's "vague sense of guilt" describes not merely his suspicion that the accumulation of the family fortune involved an act of theft, but also his recognition that it was accumulated at all. The specter that haunts Clennam's inheritance is not simply the rumor that it is constituted in part by a particular kind of appropriation, that in "grasping at money, someone may have been grievously deceived, injured, ruined," but a more general apprehension that is expressed but not comprehended by his suspicion of a particular theft. That his fortune was "grasp[ed]" is all Clennam knows when he states his willingness to "lay down all he has": the acquired character of Clennam's inheritance is sufficient to render him ready to relinquish it. His stepmother accurately accuses Clennam of identifying "the goods of this world, which [his parents] have painfully got together" (40) as "so much plunder" that must be "given up, as reparation and restitution" (40). Clennam's willingness to "lay down all he has" is less a matter of filial ingratitude than a willingness to play by a rule of equivalent exchange which ensures that the portability of property never rests.

Little Dorrit's sensitivity to the rule of exchange works to translate its positive term into its opposite: such sensitivity condemns any acquired property to an eventual loss as sure as the night that follows day; like dust to dust, anything that was once in circulation must be returned there. Adherence to this rule assumes various forms: the moral imperative that moves Arthur Clennam; the lemminglike delirium of financial speculation that moves everyone in the novel who has gotten anything to cast it all back into the river of gain and loss from whence it came; a death-driven compulsion to sell off acquired riches as inescapable as the consciousness of time.

> When he had been sinking . . . for two or three days, she observed him
> to be troubled by the ticking of his watch. . . . At length he roused him-
> self to explain that he wanted money to be raised on this watch. He was
> quite pleased when she pretended to take it away for the purpose, and
> afterwards had a relish for his little tastes of wine and jelly, that he had
> not had before. (544)

This rule makes all acquired property as haunted as the house of Merdle,
the merchant prince, whose fortune is no more than the tally of a debt:
"So modest was Mr. Merdle withal, in the midst of these splendid
achievements, that he looked far more like a man in possession of his
house under a distraint, than a commercial Colossus bestriding his own
hearthrug" (466).

All this extends beyond *Little Dorrit*: the economy of the novel represents a broader cultural complex the way that an exaggeration can
clarify what it overstates. The rule that anything received must be paid
for covers the globe according to an influential school of anthropology
associated with Marcel Mauss, whose essay on the economics of "archaic
societies" apprehends the giving of gifts as an element in a system of
exchange defined by its apparent distance from exchange. Various heirs
and critics of Mauss have argued that those aspects of his work which
encourage a conception of "archaic" economies as market logic by
another name, a conception of any expenditure that appears aloof from
motives of repayment as a matter of deceit or mystification,[5] suppress
a recognition of cultural practices that fail to conform to a narrowly
Western conviction that exchange rules the world.[6] Annette B. Weiner,
reading back from the accounts of modern anthropology, finds such
projections of the exchange imperative in the work of Marx, Mor-
gan, Durkheim, and Maine from which Mauss and his followers take
their cues:

> For these early theorists, there was little knowledge other than mission-
> aries' and travellers' sketchy accounts of how economics actually
> worked in "primitive" societies. But those projected images of reci-
> procity as the basis for an equitable economics in which Western socie-
> ties had originally participated were widely agreed upon.[7]

In the imagination of its subjects, the golden rule of market culture both
expands and intensifies. Extended outward by the projections of modern anthropology, the law of exchange is also concentrated within the
psyche of those it holds under its spell.

2

"In the very self-same course of time" (61) that *Little Dorrit* dissolves the stabilizing distance between the position of the heir and the flow of exchange, it describes all kinds of plots to reproduce this distance. Such plots typically take form as a conspiracy of good and bad cops, or capital and labor, in which one partner gets what the other owns. Christopher Casby's "grubber" comprehends only the work of acquisition: "What else do you suppose I think I am made for? Nothing. . . . Keep me always at it. . . . I have an inclination to get money, sir" (136). Pancks embodies the fury and force of this work:

> Haranguing the [tenants] . . . in their backslidings in respect of payment, demanding his bond . . . running down backsliders, sending a swell of terror on before him, and leaving it in his wake . . . Mr. Pancks wouldn't hear of excuses . . . wouldn't hear of anything but unconditional money down. Perspiring and puffing and darting about in eccentric directions, and becoming hotter and dingier every moment. (232–33)

And it is commonly assumed by the residents of Bleeding Heart Yard that Christopher Casby, the "Proprietor" (668), knows nothing of what Pancks does. His calm benevolence measures the gentleman proprietor's distance from the heat of his grubber:

> Everybody else within the bills of mortality was hot; but the Patriarch was perfectly cool. Everybody was thirsty, and the Patriarch was drinking. There was a fragrance of limes or lemons about him; and he made a drink of golden sherry, which shone in a large tumbler, as if he were drinking the evening sunshine . . . he had a radiant appearance of having in his extensive benevolence made the drink for the human species, while he himself wanted nothing but his own milk of human kindness. (664–65)

The proprietor appears to consume nothing that lies outside the confines of his estate, instead relying on his own excretions. This mirage operates to render Casby's acquisition covert even when he dines at home: "Everything about the Patriarchal household promoted quiet digestion . . . he disposed of an immense quantity of solid food with the benignity of a good soul who was feeding someone else" (131–32).

Casby's disengagement from the dinner table matches his apparent disconnection from the acquisitive labor of his grubber, since he actually directs and enforces this work from behind the scenes: "A very bad day's work, Pancks, very bad day's work. It seems to me, sir, and I must insist on making the observation forcibly . . . that you ought to have got much more money" (283). Thus Pancks undoes a simple mystification when, before the gathering of the tenants, he reveals ownership's reliance on acquisition:

> The population of the Yard was astonished at the meeting, for the two powers had never been seen there together, within the memory of the oldest Bleeding Heart. . . . "I have discharged myself from your service," said Pancks, "that I may tell you what you are. You're one of a lot of impostors. . . . You're a driver in disguise, a screwer by deputy, a wringer, a squeezer, and shaver by substitute. . . . You're a shabby deceiver." (667)

A similar segregation of owning and getting marks the relation between Little Dorrit and her father. Like Casby's grubber, Little Dorrit incarnates acquisitive activity, appearing at first in the novel as an anonymous wage laborer in Clennam's house: "Punctual to the moment, Little Dorrit appeared; punctual to the moment, Little Dorrit vanished. What became of Little Dorrit between the two eights, was a mystery" (45).

William Dorrit's dependence on what he gets from his daughter paradoxically fuels his claim of affiliation with a class that inherits rather than appropriates what it has: "The more dependent he became on the contributions of his changing family, the greater stand he made by his forlorn gentility" (61). In order to avoid upsetting her father's "genteel fiction" (61), Little Dorrit must conceal his dependence on her labor: "There's polish! . . . Miss Dorrit and her sister dursn't let him know that they work for a living" (116).

"With the same hand that had pocketed a collegian's half-crown half an hour ago, he would wipe away the tears that streamed over his cheeks if any reference were made to his daughters' earning their bread" (61). The segregation of getting and owning is here the difference between two hands ignorant of one another—what is elsewhere figured as the discrepancy between the "public character" of the Father of the Marshalsea and the emissary who takes money for him:

> "I forgot to leave this," the collegian would usually return, "for the Father of the Marshalsea." "My good sir", he would rejoin, "he is infinitely obliged to you." But to the last, the irresolute hand of old would remain in the pocket into which he had slipped the money, during two or three turns about the yard, lest the transaction should be too conspicuous. (154)

Here, the Father of the Marshalsea's disconnection from getting is a division not between himself and his hardworking daughter, but rather a division within himself, between the public character for whom the tribute is offered and his emissary who gets it. Just as he denies his dependence on the labor of Little Dorrit, the Father of the Marshalsea asserts his difference from the figure who takes alms on his behalf.

When her theft of Little Dorrit's annuity is exposed and her claim to inherited property compromised, Mrs. Clennam repeats the claim that she did not take what she owns. A sublime version of the difference between proletariat and property owner appears in Mrs. Clennam's account of the harsh, Weberian God who gets her property for her:

> When . . . I found my husband . . . to have sinned against the Lord and outraged me by holding a guilty creature in my place, was I to doubt that it had been appointed to me to make the discovery, and that it was appointed to me to lay the hand of punishment upon that creature of perdition? . . . I was appointed to find the old letter that referred to them . . . I was appointed to be the instrument of their punishment . . . I vindictive and implacable? It may seem so, to such as you who know no . . . appointment except Satan's. (647–68)

In gaining possession of the fortune that was intended for Arthur Clennam's real mother, Mrs. Clennam claims to follow divine determination, which her account figures as a matter of *appointment*: "To declare, in exercise of an authority conferred for that purpose, the destination of specific property" (*Oxford English Dictionary*). Mrs. Clennam defends her possession of property that was appointed to someone else by asserting that the act of acquisition that made it hers was the work of another. Like the truculent debt collector and the saintly woman-child, Mrs. Clennam's Calvinist deity contains the work of getting and thus offers a form of possession that retakes the heir's distance from the work of acquisition.

In each of these cases, the partition separating owning and getting collapses as soon as the complicity between them is brought to light. Pancks exposes Casby as the real subject of acquisition ("Pancks is only the Works; but here's the Winder!"); William Dorrit's ignominy leaks out in the various ways that he admits he knows what everyone else knows about his dependence on the labor of his daughter; and Mrs. Clennam's Calvinist convictions about the legitimacy of her possession are cast by the novel as a thinly disguised projection.

But while *Little Dorrit* narrates the failure of individual schemes to produce a sphere of ownership disengaged from the activity of acquisition, the topography of the novel works to describe a less fragile version of this space. Paradoxically, the novel reestablishes a realm of ownership removed from the work of getting in the very act of exposing the falsity of the proprietor's claim of distance from this activity:

[Clennam] was aware of motes and specks of suspicion, in the atmosphere of that time; seen through which medium, Christopher Casby was a mere Inn signpost without any Inn—an invitation to rest and be thankful, when there was no place to put up at, and nothing whatever to be thankful for. He knew that some of these specks even represented Christopher as capable of harboring designs in "that head," and as being a crafty impostor. . . . It was said that his being town agent to Lord Tite Barnacle was referable, not to his having the least business capacity, but to his looking so supremely benignant that nobody could suppose the property screwed or jobbed under such a man; also, that for similar reasons he now got more money out of his own wretched lettings, unquestioned than anybody with a less knobby and less shining crown could possibly have done. In a word, it was represented . . . that many people select their models, much as the painters, just now mentioned ["He had been accosted in the streets, and respectfully solicited to become a Patriarch for painters and for sculptors" (121–22)], select theirs; and that, whereas in the Royal Academy some evil old Ruffian of a Dogstealer will annually be found embodying all the cardinal virtues, on account of his eyelashes, or his chin, or his legs . . . so, in the great social Exhibition, accessories are often accepted in lieu of the internal character. (124)

The proprietor's aloofness from the work of getting is nothing but "shabby deception": "Nobody could suppose the property screwed or jobbed under such a man . . . he now got more money out of his own wretched lettings unquestioned." But what *Little Dorrit* takes away with one hand it gives back with the other: even while it dissolves the distance between Casby's ownership of the property and the work of getting it, the novel offers a different version of this separation. Casby is a proprietor uninvolved with acquisition to the extent that he is taken to be a subject for painters, a purely fictive entity, "a mere Inn signpost without any Inn." By calling the proprietor a fiction, the novel reenacts the removal that it refuses Casby when it calls him a sham: it is the mirage of the proprietor rather than Christopher Casby who reproduces the character of the heir. The fictional character of the claim of disengagement from the work of getting works less to cancel this claim than to change its locale, designating fiction itself as the site removed from acquisition; an illusion *of* distinction casts illusion *as* distinction.

This is part of a more general geography: throughout the novel, the heir's province is reinstated in the fabric of the novel itself. Little Dorrit merges with a form of fiction in the second part of the novel, when, at the urging of her father, she casts off her status as wage laborer by joining an aristocracy of painterly surfaces. While the Dorrits live off the labor of their youngest member in "Poverty," her work on their behalf becomes embarrassing in "Riches." Her father's effort to expunge all traces of acquisitive activity from Little Dorrit take shape as an attempt to make her a mirage. The translation of the wage laborer into the aristocrat's daughter is her "formation" as "a surface . . . the graceful equanimity of surface which is so expressive of good breeding" (398). Like the portraits of "noble Venetians" to whom the heir's brother "paid his court with great exactness" (401), the "surface" where Little Dorrit is made to dwell is the site of "good breeding." The "departed glory" (401) of aristocracy is landed again in painterly surfaces.

Like the "Inn signpost without any Inn," this surface aristocracy is fictional; it is defined by its disconnection from the real. The portraits of Venetian gentry attract Frederick Dorrit "merely as pictures" (401) or because "he confusedly identified them with a glory that was departed" (401). Both conceptions of the portraits assert their distance from external reference: they are either "mere pictures" or images of "*departed* glory." And if on one hand the "unrealities" (388, my emphasis) that surround the Dorrits in Venice are affiliated with aristocracy, "the real," on the other hand, is identified with the labors of getting. "Pillared galleries" and "painted chambers" make way for "beggars of all sorts everywhere": "Pitiful, picturesque, hungry, merry: children beggars and aged beggars. Often at posting houses, and other halting places, these miserable creatures would appear to her the only realities of the day" (388). Thus a division within Dickens's narrative succeeds where the plots of its characters fail: the novel reproduces the boundary between getting and owning as the difference between the fiction of breeding and the fact of beggars; between a "merely pict[orial]" court of nobility and a reality of acquisitive activity.

3

Little Dorrit restores the compromised realm of inheritance not only by reproducing versions of ownership that are defined by their distance from the work of acquisition, but also by constructing a realm of domestic relations that furnishes the object for such an owner: inherited estate is reincarnated in the woman "held" to her husband's "heart" and "locked" (681) in her husband's arms. This treasure consists not of real estate, whether defined by the walls of a house or the shape of a body, but rather of a ghost, a rhetorical form defined by its removal from its referent.

In *The Origins of the Family, Private Property and the State* (1884), Engels connects the conscription of women in monogamous marital relations with the security of private property. Describing the transition from what he regards as the historically prior "matriarchal gens" to the "pairing" family, Engels argues that the more primitive arrangement "reveals a social bond without individual possession," while the "pairing" family is a social bond that supplies the instrument for stabilizing private possession. Here is Rosalind Coward's summary of Engels:

> It is the pairing family which provides private property with a calculating agency, the monogamous family, with its supposed exigency of natural, that is, genetic, inheritance. This alone provides the motor for the emergence of structures of private property. . . . The emergence of the monogamous family constructed an economic unit of property which previously had not existed: "The transition to private property is gradually accomplished parallel with the transition . . . into monogamy."[8]

Coward objects to Engels's account because it is "steeped in the errors of speculative anthropology which assume that a general and universal history of the family was possible." But if *The Origins of the Family* fails to furnish an accurate history of the emergence of private property, it succeeds in expressing a conviction about a connection between these things which links it with Dickens's novel. I am interested in Engels's speculation not as an objective history of the rise of property, but as a text that, like *Little Dorrit*, associates the institution of marriage with the stabilization of possession. According to Engels, wives secure property by making possible its transmission through inheritance. While they are the instrument of stable property in *The Origins of the Family*, wives are the most celebrated instance of stable possession in *Little Dorrit*, where marriage replaces rather than originates inheritance.

But the husband's property does not easily transcend the terms of exchange: his wife must be *made* his and the work that makes her so must be hidden. Just as Clennam and Little Dorrit prepare to wed by destroying the "folded paper" that documents the fact that his fortune includes property taken from her, the act of appropriation that makes her his fortune is carefully obscured by the narrative. Clennam's possession of Little Dorrit takes place through an act of acquisition that we can construe only in retrospect. Like the property that is already fenced off when the founder of Civil Society ("the first person who, having fenced off a plot of ground took it into his head to say 'this is mine'") declared his possession of it in Rousseau's account, Clennam's embrace of Little Dorrit has already occurred when it is seen for the first time. She is "locked in his arms, held to his heart" (681), but the clasp that made her so is elided. All that remains for the reader to witness is the announcement of possession: "I am rich in being taken by you" (681).

This announcement appears after Little Dorrit declares that her fortune, like Clennam's own, has been swept away in the flow of circulation figured by the rise and fall of Merdle, the novel's merchant prince: "I have nothing in the world. I am as poor as when I lived here . . . papa . . . confided everything he had to [Merdle's] hands, and it is all swept away" (681). Divested of all property that is subject to gain or loss, the lovers are left with inalienable treasure. For Clennam, this possession is the woman he loves: "Never to part, my dearest Arthur; never any more until the last! . . . I am rich in being taken by you. . . . I am yours anywhere, everywhere! I love you dearly!" (681). And Little Dorrit's inalienable wealth, in turn, is to be possessed: Stripped of her fortune, she is "rich" in "being taken" by the man she adores. If Clennam is the subject who already possesses, Little Dorrit is the object already "possessed," the "being" already "taken."

Clennam's possession of the woman now "locked in his arms" is predicated on an earlier exchange in which he first acquired and then relinquished a different woman. It is after he has discharged the debt he has incurred by this prior acquisition that Clennam appears to discover rather than appropriate the woman who is the final fortune of his desire:

> To review his life, was like descending a green tree in fruit and flower, and seeing all the branches wither and drop off one by one, as he came down towards them.
>
> "From the unhappy suppression of my youngest days . . . down to the afternoon of this day with poor Flora," said Arthur Clennam, "what have I found!" His door was softly opened, and these spoken words startled him, and came as if they were an answer: "Little Dorrit." (140)

At the end of his term in debtor's prison, William Dorrit declares his intention to repay all that he owes: "Everybody . . . shall be remembered. I will not go away from here in anybody's debt" (351). Although Clennam's ruining review dismembers a green past rather than restoring borrowed money, it is a similar settling of accounts: the destruction of his old love, the withering of "poor Flora," is Clennam's way of repaying the debt that he incurred by acquiring her in the first place:

> In his youth he had ardently loved this woman, and had heaped upon her all the locked-up wealth of his affection and imagination. That wealth had been, in his desert home, like Robinson Crusoe's money; exchangeable with no one, lying idle in the dark to rust, until he poured it out for her. (125)

For Clennam, the activity of first love activates the work of exchange, the conversion of "locked-up wealth" into the currency of trade. And if Flora Finching is the recipient of Clennam's amorous capital, which "like Robinson Crusoe's money" had previously been "exchangeable with no one," she is also the property acquired through the expenditure of this currency, "exchangeable with no one . . . until he poured it out *for* her" (my emphasis). His acquisition of Flora incurs a debt that exceeds his initial outlay of "locked-up wealth" "for her"; this debt cannot be fully satisfied until he "lays down *all* he has" (268) (my emphasis)—that is, until he sacrifices the woman he has gained.

Clennam begins this restitution immediately after his primal acquisition ("Ever since that memorable time . . . he had . . . completely dismissed her" [125]), but he does not complete it until he destroys the memory that he keeps of her in "an old sacred place":

> Clennam's eyes no sooner fell upon the object of his old passion, than it shivered and broke to pieces. Most men will be found sufficiently true to themselves to be true to an old idea . . . when the idea will not bear close comparison with the reality . . . the contrast is a fatal shock to it . . . though he had . . . as completely dismissed her from any association with his Present or Future as if she had been dead . . . he had kept the old fancy of the Past unchanged, in its old sacred place. And now, after all, the last of the Patriarchs coolly walked into the parlor, saying in effect, "Be good enough to throw it down and dance upon it. This is Flora." (125)

But the final finding of Clennam's desire evades the demands of exchange. Something is ultimately left over in the economy of love: in the end, it is not necessary for the guilt-ridden heir to lay down *all* he has: "Dear Mr. Clennam, don't let me see you weep! Unless you weep with pleasure to see me. . . . Your own poor child come back" (631). Little Dorrit only looks like a child, as a streetwalker who mistakes her for one discovers to her dismay: "'My God,' she said, recoiling, 'you're a woman!'" (148). The streetwalker's error measures Little Dorrit's capacity as erotic capital: Clennam can safely possess Little Dorrit because she substitutes for, rather than restores, the child love that he must relinquish in order to satisfy the requirements of equivalent exchange: "His door was softly opened, and these spoken words startled him, and came *as if* they were an answer: 'Little Dorrit'" (my emphasis). The substitution that startles Clennam is an alibi for a lost past: a kind of referentless representation forms the object of apparently unacquired property in *Little Dorrit*, just as, elsewhere in the novel, other versions of referentless representation form the subject of unacquisitive ownership. Little Dorrit can only signify rather than symbolize Clennam's prior acquisition, because the woman he actually acquired is relinquished to the demands of exchange. Nevertheless, while Clennam does not take hold of Little Dorrit, his possession of her depends on a prior acquisition. This allegorical figure succeeds as a kind of surplus value because, unlike Flora Finching, she is constituted by means of, but is not herself a part of, an exchange. Little Dorrit appears through Clennam's acquisition and consequent relinquishing of Flora Finching, but she is not actually an element of that transaction.

The crisis of ownership that occurs in *Little Dorrit* when the acquisition of property is made visible comes to an end when a lover embraces a romantic fortune that he did not appear to get and that he therefore holds securely: "Locked in his arms, held to his heart. . . . 'Never to part, my dearest Arthur; never any more until the last!'" And while such possession appears to transcend the exigencies of capitalism, it resembles more a rehearsal of its first rule: the triumph that closes the novel is the discovery of something like the capitalist principle of exploitation, the source of surplus value.

Here is Marx's account of the "peculiar nature of labour-power":

> One consequence of the peculiar nature of labour-power as a commodity is this, that it does not in reality pass straight away into the hands of the buyer on the conclusion of the contract between buyer and seller. Its [exchange] value, like that of every other commodity, is already determined before it enters into circulation, for a definite quantity of social labour has been spent in the production of the labour power. But its use-value consists in the subsequent exercise of that power. The alienation [*Versüsserung*] of labour-power and its real manifestation [*Ausserung*]; i.e. the period of its existence as a use-value, do not coincide in time.[9]

In "the subsequent exercise of that power" labor produces something that exceeds its exchange value, the cost of reproducing its needs; the surplus value that capital gains, like Clennam's embrace of Little Dorrit, is distinguished from the value that it exchanges, but, like Clennam's allegorical possession, this apparently unappropriated surplus is nevertheless contingent upon the value previously exchanged.

Thus domestic estate in the novel resembles the formation of, rather than a flight from, capital. This similarity between the property of the capitalist in Marx's account and the lover's fortune in *Little Dorrit* becomes dramatic when Little Dorrit reveals her love to be labor power: "I am yours anywhere, everywhere! I love you dearly! I would rather pass my life here with you, and go out daily, working for our bread, than I would have the greatest fortune that ever was told" (681).

Such fortune is man's estate: the difference between Clennam's allegorical wealth and "the Shadow of Someone" that a "tiny woman" keeps as her "great, great treasure" in a fairy tale Little Dorrit tells makes this clear. At first, Little Dorrit's fairy tale appears to indicate that the possibility of allegorical possession is available to anyone, that a woman can possess without appearing to acquire a displaced version of a man in the erotic economy of *Little Dorrit*, just as a man possesses a displaced version of a woman. But the novel draws a distinction between masculine and feminine versions of such property: while Clennam's erotic fortune is a form of surplus value, the tiny woman's shadow hoard is a fantasy of possession.

In Little Dorrit's narrative, the "tiny woman" who harbors "the shadow of Someone who had gone by long before" is confronted by a princess:

> The Princess was such a wonderful Princess that she had the power of knowing secrets, and she said to the tiny woman, "Why do you keep it there?" This showed her directly that the Princess knew why she lived all alone by herself. . . . It was the shadow of Someone who had gone by long before: of Someone who had gone on far away quite out of reach, never, never, to come back. It was brighter to look at; and when the tiny woman showed it to the Princess, she was proud of it with all her heart, as a great, great, treasure. When the Princess had considered it a little while, she said to the tiny woman, "And you keep watch over this every day?" And she cast down her eyes, and whispered, "Yes." The Princess said, "Remind me why." To which the other replied, that no one so good and kind had ever passed that way, and that was why in the

beginning. She said too, that nobody missed it, that nobody was the worse for it, that Someone had gone on to those who were expecting him . . . and that this remembrance was stolen, or kept back from nobody. (245)

The woman's treasure is removed from the movement of circulation described by the path of "Someone who had gone on far away quite out of reach." Unable to acquire Someone when he is within "reach," the humble cottager does not mourn his loss when he is gone. Instead, she harbors his shadow, a belated representation that appears uninvolved in the movement of gain and loss. Her proud proprietorship resembles the condition of her interlocutor; like the princess, who has knowledge without appearing to get it, the tiny woman has the shadow of someone without appearing to engage in the work of acquiring it: "Nobody missed it, . . . nobody was the worse for it . . . this remembrance was stolen, or kept back from nobody."

The shadow property offers the appearance of a possession that is not taken, and this appearance constitutes its inalienability for the cottager:

> This remembrance was stolen or kept back from nobody. The Princess made answer, Ah! But when the cottager died it would be discovered there. The tiny woman told her No; when that time came, it would sink quietly into her own grave, and would never be found. . . . [When the cottager died t]he Princess . . . went . . . to search for the treasured shadow. But there was no sign of it to be found anywhere; and then she knew that the tiny woman had told her the truth, and that it . . . had sunk quietly into her own grave, and that she and it were at rest together. (246)

While Someone has "gone on far away quite out of reach," his shadow appertains to the tiny woman as apparently unacquired and thus inalienable property that disappears only with her death. Here again, representation, rather than real estate, is the form of property secure from the destabilizing force of commodification; here again, the stability of inheritance is replaced by a shadow of prior fortune.

But unlike the allegorical term that constitutes Clennam's secure estate, the consolation of the humbler cottager is an object of representation ("the shadow of Someone") that substitutes for an original object that *was not* gotten ("Someone . . . who had gone on far away quite out of reach"), rather than an object that was taken and then released. Here, the allegorical term does not appear as the shadow of a previously acquired and relinquished primary object; rather, it furnishes a kind of property that stands in for an original object that could not be had in the first place.

Little Dorrit's cottager inhabits a spatial and temporal margin outside and after a system of circulation inscribed by the movement of "Someone who had gone by long before: of Someone who had gone on far away quite out of reach . . . Someone had gone on to those who were expecting him." The humble cottager proudly possesses a shadow treasure instead of what she would have had if she were able to make a place for herself on a path of circulation that excludes her.

If Clennam's possession of allegorical surplus value is predicated on earlier acquisition and loss of primary property, the cottager's shadow hoard is predicated on the absence of this prior involvement in the work of exchange. Clennam's erotic estate appears after the discharging of this work; the cottager's shadow treasure signals her exclusion from it. In *Little Dorrit*, property removed from the flow of circulation by its secondary character furnishes in a form of surplus value the security of the heir to the anxious capitalist. But for a woman who resides on the margins of a system of allotment, the allegorical supplies consolation for an unchosen distance from this flow. Property distanced from circulation may be the material of a shelter or a ghetto, depending on the status of its occupant.

4

Among the "traces of the migratory habits of the family" housed in the Meagleses' snug bourgeois domicile is a collection of "pictorial acquisitions" procured during their tours abroad:

> Of articles collected on his various expeditions, there was such a vast miscellany that it was like the dwelling of an amiable Corsair. . . . There were views, like and unlike, of a multitude of places; and there was one little picture-room devoted to a few of the regular sticky old Saints. . . . Of these pictorial acquisitions Mr. Meagles spoke in the usual manner. He was no judge, he had picked them up, dirt-cheap, and people *had* considered them rather fine. One man, who at any rate ought to know something of the subject, had declared that "Sage, Reading" . . . to be a fine Guercino. (163)

In the novel's description of these paintings, the corsair's acquisition of spectacle gives way to the spectacle of acquisition:

A few of the regular sticky old Saints, with . . . hair like Neptune's, wrinkles like tattooing, and coats of varnish . . . [which] served for a fly-trap, and became what is now called in the vulgar tongue a Catch-em-alive O . . . a specially oily old gentleman, with a swan's-down tippet for a beard, and a web of cracks all over him like rich pie crust. (163)

If these are figures of acquisitive activity, they are also allusions to the range of the feminine anatomy in Dickens's novels. The images and agents of getting that occupy the surfaces of Meagles's paintings cover the range of Dickens's ideas about women: "Rich pie crust" serves as a metonymy for homey virtues; "varnish" describes the consorts of social corruption. But in league with the work of getting, these allusions undergo nightmare distortions. As acquisitive capacity, the feminine ceases to be good, or merely false, and becomes instead a form of genitalia that scars and "stick[s]."

Acquisitiveness is a "*view*" when it appears in the shape of a vagina that wounds and ensnares (my emphasis). In the web of cracks and the figure of the flytrap, *Little Dorrit* intimates the panic caused there by a "perverse" and unabashedly acquisitive woman. They suggest, that is, the figure of Miss Wade, a "myster[ious]" (277) female who casts the relation between men and women in terms that recall Clennam's primal desire for spending and getting, instead of a later passion that seems disengaged from the demands of exchange. Miss Wade's account of her own betrothal characterizes it as a transaction that Clennam's possession of Little Dorrit appears to transcend:

I cannot avoid saying, he admired me; but, if I could, I would. . . . [H]is admiration worried me. He took no pains to hide it; and caused me to feel among the rich people as if he had bought me for my looks, and made a show of his purchase to justify himself. . . . [His aunt] seemed to think that her distinguished nephew had gone into a slave-market and purchased a wife. (558, 560)

Wade's alliance with Tattycoram, the Meagleses' alienated, alienable servant girl, "is founded in a common cause. What your broken plaything is as to birth, I am" (278). According to Wade, her fellow orphan woman, like Wade herself, is acquired rather than natural property:

Here is your patron, your master. He is willing to take you back. . . . You can be again, a foil to his pretty daughter, a slave to her pleasant wilfulness, and a toy in the house showing the goodness of the family. You can have your droll name again, playfully pointing you out and setting you apart. (Your birth, you know; you must not forget your birth.) You can again be shown to this gentleman's daughter, Harriet, and kept before her, as a living reminder of her own superiority and gracious condescension. (276)

Tattycoram's status as a slave in Meagles's house is measured by the fact that her origin is elsewhere—what "set[s her] apart" from the "gentleman's daughter," according to Wade, is her "birth." Like the "spoils" (163) that Meagles shows his guests before he leads them to his "own snug room" (164), Tattycoram "stops outside the door" (164) of both the father's filial estate and the lover's erotic museum. In contrast to the natural property of a father or the souvenir of a lover, the orphan laborer is explicitly acquired by her "master" and is thus "portable property," located within a system of circulation that surfaces again when "Miss Wade . . . put her arm around her waist as if she took possession of her for evermore" (277).

Bearing witness to the acquisition of women, and acquiring one herself, Miss Wade makes the work of exchange visible in a sphere that the novel and its characters seek to remove from its destabilizing demands. The ominous form of her femininity is affiliated with a transgression that briefly disturbs the security of phallic estate:

"I am alone here, gentlemen," observed Miss Wade. . . . "Say anything you will."

"Politeness must yield to this misguided girl, ma'am," said Mr. Meagles, "at her present pass; though I hope not altogether to dismiss it, even with the injury you do her so strongly before me. Excuse me for reminding you in her hearing—I must say it—that you were a mystery to all of us, and had nothing in common with any of us, when she unfortunately fell in your way. I don't know what you are, but you don't hide, can't hide, what a dark spirit you have within you. If it should happen that you are a woman, who, from whatever cause, has a perverted delight in making a sister-woman as wretched as she is (I am old enough to have heard of such) I warn her against you, and I warn you against yourself." (277)

The word that Meagles uses against Miss Wade's relationship with Tattycoram is the one that the novel invokes to describe the subversion of the boundary that separates acquisitive activity from what normally falls outside it. According to Little Dorrit, her family "pervert[s]" (219) Maggy when they send her to get money from Clennam, since this compromises the dutiful daughter's efforts to contain acquisitive activity: "If we should want it so very, very badly that we cannot do without it, let *me* ask . . . for it" (145). Wade's "delight" in "making a sister woman as wretched as she is" perversely transgresses the boundary that appears elsewhere in the novel to construct the feminine as a form of apparently unacquired property.

In *Little Dorrit*, the delight of perversity is the sign of poverty. Like the heroine of the fairy tale who apprehends a previous arrangement that prohibits her from having the object of her desire ("Someone had gone on to those who were expecting him"), Wade recognizes an impoverishing circumstance that prevents her from "securing" what she wants in either explicitly economic or domestic spheres. Having inherited insufficient property to sustain herself, Wade is compelled to work as a governess. Her account of this labor culminates in her recognition that she cannot "secure" the affection of her charges:

> I liked the children. They were timid, but on the whole disposed to attach themselves to me. There was a nurse, however, in the house, a rosy-faced woman . . . who had nursed them both, and who had secured their affections before I saw them. (556)

Unlike Clennam, whose loss of capital is his access to secure domestic fortune, Wade is ineligible for either form of allotment.

The act of "t[aking]" a woman is visible only in and to a woman who has felt a desire to do so defeated. While Clennam's acquisition of Little Dorrit is effaced, the desire of a woman for a woman is made conscious by its failure: "When we were left alone in our bedroom at night, I would reproach her . . . loving her as much as ever, and often feeling as if, rather than suffer so, I could hold her in my arms and plunge to the bottom of a river—where I could still hold her, after we were both dead" (555). [10]

Perversity's explicit embrace triumphs for a moment when "Miss Wade . . . put[s] her arm around [Tattycoram's] waist as if she took possession of her for evermore," but it is finally defeated when Tattycoram goes back to the Meagleses. It may be, as Wade believes, that the servant's return to her "master" (276) measures again the difference that appears between the capitalized admiration of Wade's suitor ("as if he had bought me") and her own forlorn and impoverished desire to hold another woman ("I . . . often [felt] as if, rather than suffer so, I could hold her in my arms and plunge to the bottom of a river"); it may be, as Wade believes, that the servant's return charts the greater acquisitive power of capital over other ways of getting: "You prefer their plenty to your less fat living here. . . . My poverty will not bear competition with their money" (553). But the voice of Miss Wade is lost in a reunion celebration where all traces of the servant's appropriation are absent. No longer a foreign acquisition, the "handsome girl with lustrous dark hair and eyes" (14) is now the prodigal daughter, restored to the embrace of the parents: "Father and Mother Meagles never deserved their names better, than when they took the headstrong foundling girl into their protection again" (676).

And here the spectacle of immanent franchise works twice to make appropriation covert. The returning servant girl brings with her the now-secure secret of a troubling acquisition:

> Another opening of the door, and Tattycoram subsided, and Little Dorrit came in, and Mr. Meagles with pride and joy produced the box, and her gentle face was lighted up with grateful happiness and joy. The secret was safe now! She could keep her own part of it from him; he should never know of her loss; in time to come, he should know all that was of import to himself; but he should never know what concerned her, only. (676)

The figure of restoration has for its freight the secret of acquisition, private knowledge of a theft available only to its victim.

For Your Eyes Only: Private Property and the
Oriental Body in *Dombey and Son*

1

A FAMILIAR PASSAGE in *Dombey and Son* describes the limitless contours of the "one idea of" capital, the conviction that all parts of the universe are comprehended by the shape of the commodity, that the site of the "system" of capitalized exchange is pervasive.

> The earth was made for Dombey and Son to trade in, and the sun and moon were made to give them light. Rivers and seas were formed to float their ships; rainbows gave them promise of fair weather; winds blew for or against their enterprises; stars and planets circled their orbits, to preserve inviolate a system of which they were the centre. (50)[1]

Dombey's conception of the entire world as the site and accessory of capitalized trade accords with a strain of nineteenth- and twentieth-century enthusiasm within the Occident for the exportation of capitalism to the Third World, as well as various critical accounts of it.[2] Both the exponents of capitalist imperialism and its historians and theoreticians regard the globalization of capitalist trade as the tool of capitalism, casting it either as the means of spreading its splendors or as a solution for its problems.

But while Dombey conceives of the world as the theater of trade, the novel also maps a more heterogeneous geography. If Dombey regards the entire world as the site of trade, elsewhere in the novel intercourse with distant regions serves to protect various spaces within the Occident from the reach of capital.

A rumor of the relation I want to investigate here appears in the cozy domesticity of Solomon Gill's shop, whose antiquated wares are at once "ship-shape" and inaccessible to the view or grasp of customers:

> Objects in brass and glass were in his drawers and on his shelves, which none but the initiated could have found the top of, or guessed the use of, or having once examined, could have ever got back again into their

mahogany nests without assistance. Everything was jammed into the tightest cases, fitted into the narrowest corners, fenced up behind the most impertinent cushions, and screwed into the acutest angles, to prevent its philosophic composure from being disturbed by the rolling of the sea . . . so much practical navigation was fitted, and cushioned, and screwed into every box . . . that the shop itself . . . seemed almost to become a snug, sea-going, ship-shape concern, wanting only good sea-room . . . to work its way securely to any desert island in the world. (88–89)[3]

I want to suggest that we can apprehend a crucial causality in Dickens's novel if we invert the relation set forth here. Although according to this passage, the midshipman's shop is made snug and secret, its merchandise made fast in order to ready it for exotic voyages, in *Dombey and Son* such voyages are more generally the means for defending private property from apprehension and acquisition by others.

This pattern of dependency appears first in the outline of the novel's plot: if Sol Gill's wares attract no customers, they remain vulnerable nevertheless to the demands of exchange, and the protection of the shop from the bankruptcy auctioneer requires an exotic journey. Walter Gay, Gill's nephew and a lowly employee of Dombey and Son, is compelled to accept from his master a "junior situation in . . . Barbados" (243), because Dombey has protected his uncle's shop from the debt collector: "As the question of going or not going, Walter did not consider that he had any power of choice in the matter. . . . His Uncle and he lay under a great obligation to Mr Dombey . . . and duty must be done" (277).

The connection that the novel establishes between involvement with exotic places and secure estate at home may be situated in a wider historical frame. In *The Country and the City*, Raymond Williams considers the internationalization of the "traditional relationship between the country and the city"[4] brought about by the global extension of Occidental rule and capitalist trade during the eighteenth and nineteenth centuries. This expansion of Western political and economic control into the Third World not only widened the borders of the country to include colonized territories, but also instated among the officers of the empire an idealized vision of "rural England . . . its green peace contrasted with the tropical or arid places of actual work" (281). As Williams suggests, this rustic conception of England may surprise us, since "the society from which these people had come was, after all, the most urban and industrialized in the world, and it was usually in the service of just these elements that they had gone out" (282). Williams suggests that this pastoral dream was primarily an economic fantasy, or, to be more specific, a fantasy of the transcendence of the economic: "In practical terms, the reward for service, though anticipated more often than it was gained, was a return to a rural place within this urban and industrial England: the 'residential' rural England, the 'little place in the country.' . . . The country, now, was a place to retire to" (282). This brief version of landed aristocracy, a sanctuary from the activity of capitalized exchange, was cast as the reward for a career in the east.

While the midshipman's shop is not a country house, its riches are relics, and like the pastoral place, it is a form of estate retired from the noise of commerce. And just as colonial service in "the tropical or arid places" of the Third World is the price for the "little place in the country" in Williams's account, in Dickens's novel the position in Barbados is the price for protecting Uncle Sol's shop from the broker.

This dependency defines a more complicated relation described by the novel, between the safety of domestic estate and the sphere of the exotic. I will argue here that *Dombey and Son* internationalizes the effort to shelter estate from the threats of capital: the novel purifies property of the commodity's taint through a strategy of containment and catharsis that resorts to the Orient. However, before I place my argument in global terms, before I specify the character and effect of the Oriental in *Dombey and Son*, I need first to outline the condition of the local economy; I need to consider how the novel's conception of capital is antithetical to its conception of possession.

In *Dombey and Son*, to own is to own alone. "Partner[ship]" in the family firm is "reserved solely to inheritors of that great name," and this restriction is even narrower than it looks; it diminishes the number of eligible partners to one, since Dombey and Son, in the annals of the firm, are indifferent instances of a single person, the corporate proprietor who is the lone subject of house correspondence:

> He will be christened Paul . . . of course. . . . His father's name . . . and his grandfather's! . . . There is some inconvenience in the necessity of writing Junior . . . but it . . . doesn't enter into the correspondence of the House. *Its* signature remains the same. (50)

The rule of exclusive access applies as well to the "Home Department" of the firm, where Dombey's "sense of property in his child" (70) receives "a rude shock" (70) when he is compelled to share his son, even with a wet-nurse. Dombey's "haughty dread of having any rival or partner in the boy's respect and deference" (103) registers the rigidity of the right of property in *Dombey and Son*.

This conception of ownership appears most vividly in the light of its failure, the funereal light of a father's grief over the death of his son. Dombey's "sense of property in his child" is dissolved when the boy's corpse is converted into a joint-stock company: "Everyone set up some claim or other to a share in his dead boy, and was a bidder against him!" (353). Dombey's "sense of property in his child" is not merely (as we might expect) diluted or endangered when others claim some share in him, but altogether canceled and replaced by the necessity of bidding for what was previously his.

The strict boundaries of possession surveyed by Dombey's selfish rage measure more than the eccentricities of pathological jealousy. Rather, the definition of ownership as the right of exclusive access is an ideological construct whose force appears in our inability to imagine an alternative description of the term, in our sense that the phrase "private property" is redundant. Ownership, in the words of Miss Tox, appears to be nothing other than "exclusion itself" (159). Theorists of property such as C. B. Macpherson dispute this identification of ownership with the right of exclusive access, characterizing this conception of property as a crucial contraction of its meaning, a narrowing of the category concomitant with the ascendancy of capitalism. The canonization of private property as the sole form of possession is cast by such theorists as a construct that appears and cooperates with capitalism, situated as an integral element of an economy dominated by commodity exchange.[5]

Dickens's chronicle of the fortunes of Dombey and Son describes an economy in which the right of exclusive access is not only a condition that enables the commodity form, but also a causality of the commodity form. To see how this works in *Dombey and Son*, we need first to notice how the novel radicalizes the definition of private possession by extending the boundary of exclusion. We can apprehend the extremity of the privacy of property in *Dombey and Son* by investigating the scene of its demise. The "misfortune" that the midshipman's shop glimpses and escapes when Brogley, the bankruptcy auctioneer, seizes possession of its private treasures is the fate of the house of Dombey and Son, when the Capital Modern Household Furniture and Company appears after Dombey's disaster to auction off its contents in an orgy of exposure:

> There is not a secret place in the whole house . . . brokers invade the very fire escape, and take a panoramic survey. . . . This lasts all day and three days following. The Capital Modern Household Furniture, &c., is on sale. . . . For nearly a whole week, the Capital Modern Household Furniture, &c., is in course of removal. At last all is gone. (928–29)

This scene stages a conjunction mentioned earlier in Mr. Brogley's shop, where lost property is *put on view*, "present[ing] to the eye an eternal perspective of bankruptcy and ruin" (177). The spectacle of bankruptcy suggests the merging of spectacle and bankruptcy in *Dombey and Son*; here, property is lost when it is made public. Dickens's novel escalates the conception of ownership as exclusive access to the uses of property by extending the ensemble of those uses to include even its cognitive apprehension. If, in *Dombey and Son*, to own is to own alone, to own alone is to own in secret.

The bleakness of the House of Dombey, for example, has no exposed sound; it reflects rather the blankness that conceals and thus preserves all that belongs to Dombey: "It was as blank a house inside as outside. . . . Mr Dombey ordered the furniture to be covered up . . . to preserve it for the son" (75). A common figure of speech encapsulates the philosophy of property in *Dombey and Son*: "He is going to have . . . the books kept closer" (99). Fortune's closeness shades the novel's account of London's financial district in a chapter ironically entitled "More First Appearances." Near the offices of Dombey and Son, "the Royal Exchange was close at hand; the Bank of England, with its vaults of gold and silver 'down among the dead men' underground, was their magnificent neighbour" (87). Both the Royal Exchange, "close at hand," and the crypt that covers and protects the gold and silver of the Bank of England instate an affiliation of secrecy and security. Small fortunes, as well as large ones, are kept covertly. On the margin of fortune's district, Sol Gill's wares are secure, not only because they cannot be pried out of their ship-shape corners, but also because they cannot be seen or understood; his "old Madeira," the rare wine "long excluded from the light of day" (970), furnishes a totem for secure, because secret, property in *Dombey and Son*.

Conversely, if to "preserve" property is to "cover it up," the loss of property occurs when it is made available to the apprehension of others. It is to defend against the alienation of publication that Major Bagstock declines to mention the name of Dombey's future wife in the presence of others: "He holds that name too sacred to be made the property of these fellows, or of any fellows" (455). The loss of property in the flood-lights of publicity appears on the grandest theater when Carker, the capitalist's treacherous assistant, manages Dombey's loss of fortune not by stealing it, but by staging it:

He has . . . pampered the vanity and ambition of his employer. . . . Undertakings have been entered on to swell the reputation of the

House for vast resources, and to exhibit it in magnificent contrast to other merchants' Houses, of which it requires a steady hand to contemplate the possibly . . . ruinous consequences. (843)

Exhibition of property is again identified with its loss when Dombey's ruin is cast as an instance of the pervasive problem of "bankrupt traders . . . in shows and pretences" (909). Conspicuousness is leagued with bankruptcy in a novel where to show what you have to others is to lose it.

After his sense of property in his son is dissolved, Dombey retires with his sorrow to the site of an archaic form of possession, a "place wherein he would have lorded [his grief] alone" (353).[6] But Dombey's sense of ownership collapses again because others claim access to his property, "a herd to insult him with their knowledge of his defeated hopes, and their boasts of claiming community of feeling with himself, so far removed: if not of having crept into the place where he would have lorded it alone!"(353). Dombey is divested of his grief, "the trial and disappointment of a proud man's secret heart" (353), in a loss of psychic capital that recapitulates his loss of the corpse. While "he *would* have lorded" his melancholy within the exclusive confines of his "heart," the "claims" of others again cancel the possibility of such possession (my emphasis). Like the claims of everyone for a share in his boy, the assertion of knowledge of his defeated hopes, the "claim of community of feeling" with his grief, dissolves Dombey's melancholy estate. The death of his son thus twice "shock[s] . . . his sense of property" in him: just as the corpse is lost to the father because others claim a share in it, his melancholy cannot be his when it cannot be his secret.

Edith Dombey's disenfranchisement rehearses the novel's equation of the loss of property and the invasion of privacy. Her own hold on her "accomplishment[s] or grace[s]" is canceled when they are broadcast on the marketplace:

> I have been offered and rejected, put up and appraised, until my very soul has sickened. I have not had an accomplishment or grace that might have been a resource to me, but it has been paraded and vended to enhance my value, as if the common crier had called it through the streets. (856)

Edith posits a mutual exclusion between the character of her accomplishments and graces as resources potentially belonging to her and their exhibition in the marketplace. Since they are "paraded and vended," they cannot be a resource for her. This alienation of potential property results not from its sale, but merely from its availability for sale: Edith is divested of personal property not because it is sold, but because it is advertised.

The broadcasting that cancels the privacy of property and thus abrogates ownership clusters around a particular form in the novel, a form instantiated by Edith's exhibition on the auctioneer's block: Edith is offered—at once "put up and appraised." This phrase implies not only that the capital value of Edith's resources is exhibited, her "accomplishment[s]" and "grace[s]" "paraded and vended to enhance [her] value," but also that her translation into value that can be bought with money is itself a kind of spectacle.[7]

In all of its forms, capital is exhibition. It composes the collective speech that is the noise of the novel; its "voices" (87), the "uproar of [its] streets" (87), are the shouts of perambulating merchants and the "suggestions of precious stuffs" (87). "Suggestions" are issued *by* "precious stuffs"; "gold and silver" themselves offer "demonstration[s]" (584); "commodities [are] . . . addressed to the general public" (237). As Dombey's definition of money suggests, "a very potent spirit . . . that cause[s] us to be honoured, feared, respected . . . and ma[kes] us powerful and glorious in the eyes of all men" (152–53), capital is a means of communication that may best be described as publication.

Money is not the only form of capital that talks in *Dombey and Son*: their common character as communication unites money with forms of wealth that are more obviously symbolic, such as the "capital of the House's name" (51). In *Outline for a Theory of Practice*, Pierre Bourdieu analyzes the socially enforced distinction between "material and symbolic exchange . . . [between] circulation and communication," complicating and mitigating the separation of these spheres by pointing to their cooperation and interconvertibility.[8] Relevant here is the character of symbolic capital in Bourdieu's account as *symbolic*, that is, its character as communication. The transactions that Bourdieu calls symbolic exchange, transactions apparently removed from the sphere of "material exchange," such as gift-giving, are always gestures of address. I want to suggest that Dickens's novel radicalizes to the point of identity the intimacy between symbolic and material capital. Here, "material and symbolic exchange" are not merely interconvertible, they are two ways of saying the same thing:

> "Carker," said Mr Dombey, "I am sensible that you do not limit your—"
>
> "Service," suggested his smiling entertainer.
>
> "No; I prefer to say your regard," observed Mr Dombey; very sen-

sible, as he said so, that he was paying him a handsome and flattering compliment, "to our mere business relations." (681)

The capacity of both money and the "capital of the House's name" to exact "regard" dissolves the difference between the form of capital inhabiting a "mere business relation" between employer and employee (the wages that purchase Carker's "service") and "symbolic capital." If in this exchange communication is cast as a kind of capital ("he was paying him a handsome and flattering compliment"), all kinds of capital are cast as communication in *Dombey and Son*.

Capital is a sign, not a substance; the "image" of the "Son of the Firm" is indistinguishable from the "impression" that it communicates: "If there were a warm place in [Dombey's] frosty heart, his son occupied it; if its very hard surface could receive the impression of any image, the image of that son was there . . . as the 'Son' of the Firm" (151).

Similarly, the novel defines the "vast resources" of Dombey and Son endangered by Carker's exhibition of them as the "credit" of the house, and thus describes the capital displayed by Carker as an instance, rather than the object, of communication. As Sol Gills suggests, Dombey and Son consists of "bankers' books, or cheque books, or bills, or such tokens of wealth rolling in from day to day" (92).[9]

Recent histories of the commodity's spectacular abilities of expression date their origin in the Victorian period and point to the involvement of new industries of advertising, whose modern forms get off the ground during the latter half of the nineteenth century. Thomas Richards and Jennifer Wicke have noticed that the commodity's developing capacities of expression, a gain of semiotic volume that accompanied and helped to achieve its gain in material volume,[10] were assisted by new strategies of advertisement. But as Wicke suggests, the publicity that advertising accorded the commodity form has its prehistory, one that precedes the great campaigns of the second half of the nineteenth century, one written earlier into the very form of the commodity itself, as it is described by the midcentury novel. In a book like *Dombey and Son*, the commodity form doesn't need the agency of advertising to make itself known; its native talents are their own publicity. According to the view of the Dickens novel, the commodity is not merely advertised or exhibited; it is itself already advertisement and exhibition.

The "bankrupt[cy]" of those whose only property consists of "shows and pretenses" is a common destitution, a pervasive poverty that afflicts any owner of capital. Such ownership is a self-canceling term in *Dombey and Son*, since capital is exhibition and as such dismantles the boundary of secrecy that defines possession in the novel. The alienation of Dombey's filial property in a flood of publicity is not an accident; rather, it results from the boy's character as part of the "capital of the House's name," the "'Son' of the Firm." The "capital" that is the "Firm's name" is "known and honoured in the British possessions abroad" (188); and if, in the words of one sycophant, "no one can be a stranger to Mr Dombey's influence," the horde that divests Dombey of his private sorrow indicates that no one can be kept a stranger to Dombey's estate.[11]

This horde is led by Toodle, the husband of the dead boy's wet-nurse, who presumes to share in Dombey's grief by wearing a sign of mourning for Paul: "So from high to low . . . from Florence in his great house to the coarse churl who was feeding the fire then smoking before them, everyone set up some claim or other to a share in his dead boy." Toodle approaches the grieving financier, who had earlier expressed his contempt for the laborer's ignorance, because he is anxious to announce his improvement:

> "And in the matter o' readin'," said Toodle, ducking again, as if to remind Mr Dombey of what had passed between them on that subject long ago, "them boys o' mine, they learned me, among 'em, arter all. They've made a wery tolerable scholar of me, Sir, them boys." (352)

The now-literate Toodle stands for "everyone," the all-inclusive population who "set up some claim or other to a share in his dead boy": "everyone's share" in the dead boy is, more specifically, every *reader's* share. Dickens announces as much in his preface to *Dombey and Son* when he speaks of the novel's fabulously popular account of Paul Dombey's death: "If any of . . . my readers . . . have felt a sorrow in one of the principal incidents on which this fiction turns, I hope it may be a sorrow of that sort which endears the sharers in it" (41).

Dombey's interest in the progress of the "Son of the firm," part of the "capital" of the firm's name and "title" (937), is the fascination of the novel reader:

> [Dombey] loved his son with all the love he had. If there were a warm place in his frosty heart, his son occupied it; if its very hard surface could receive the impression of any image, the image of that son was there; though not so much as an infant, or as a boy, but as a grown man—the "Son" of the Firm. Therefore he was impatient to advance into the future, and to hurry over the intervening passages of his history. (151)

The capital that is the name of the house is identified as a novel, a "history," much like *Dombey and Son* itself, I suppose, whose extreme length (Dickens's longest work) might tempt an "impatient" reader to "hurry over [its] intervening passages." Historians of the novel have characterized the form as a mode of literary production constituted by a mass-market audience.[12] Like the clamor of commodities that inhabit it, the novel itself is a kind of commodified speech addressed to the general public. And if *Dombey and Son* is like capital, capital, in *Dombey and Son*, is like the novel. This affiliation describes the breadth of capital's availability: the capital of the house is available to anyone who can read its name, both within the bounds of the novel and beyond.[13]

2

In keeping with the commonplace Victorian designation of the domestic sphere as a sanctuary from commerce, *Dombey and Son* establishes, within "the Home Department," a space for covert possession, sheltered from the alienating floodlights of capital. The novel's domestic estate includes Florence's "sense of property" in the love that she feels for her father ("she . . . hoarded up her undivided secret in the mournful house" [694]), and the retired capitalist's hoard at the end of the novel:

> No one . . . knows the measure of the white-haired gentleman's affection for the girl. That story never goes about. The child herself almost wonders at a certain secrecy he keeps in it. He hoards her in his heart. . . . He is fondest of her and most loving to her, when there is no creature by. (975)

These domestic properties prepare for and attend the hoarding of Florence herself, the "undivided treasure" of Walter Gay. After her engagement to him, Florence, in an agoraphobic delirium,

> never left her high rooms but to steal downstairs to wait for [Gay] when it was time to come, or, sheltered by his proud, encircling arm, to bear him company to the door again, and sometimes peep into the street. Oh blessed time! Oh wandering heart at rest! Oh deep, exhaustless, mighty well of love, in which so much was sunk! (883–84)

Sequestered within the private space of her fiancé's "high rooms" or by his "encircling" arm, Florence is prepared for her nuptial encryption.

Florence's wedding path is a progressively "dark and narrow street"

49

(902) that leads her away from the light of the sun to "the darkening mist of the City." The activity of appearance that adorns the bridal sojourn at its outset ("the sun shines on them"; "riches are uncovering"; "jewels, gold, and silver flash") is diminished and made passive as it progresses:

> Gradually they come into the darker, narrower streets, where the sun, now yellow, and now red, is seen through the mist, only at street corners, and in small open spaces where there is a tree . . . or a burying ground, where the few tombs and tombstones are almost black. (902)

Disappearing light is replaced by the figure of the crypt, both along the way of Florence's wedding walk and at the end of it, as the end of it:

> The air is darkened and she is trembling in a church which has a strange smell like a cellar. . . . Youthful, and how beautiful, the young bride looks, in this old dusty place, with no kindred object near her but her husband. There is a dusty old clerk, who keeps a sort of evaporated news shop underneath an archway opposite behind a perfect fortification of posts. . . . There is a dusty old beadle . . . who has something to do with a Worshipful Company who have got a Hall in the next yard, with a stained glass window in it that no mortal ever saw. . . . There are dusty old sounding-boards over the pulpit and reading-desk, looking like lids to be let down on the officiating ministers in case of their giving offence. . . . No gracious ray of light is seen to fall on Florence. . . . The morning luminary is built out, and don't shine there. (902–3)

The encrypted bride joins the "old Madeira" in the cellar, as treasure "excluded from the light of day"; the girl whom Gay marries, like the wine that Sol Gills sequesters, is secure, covert estate. On the eve of their marriage, Florence stages a fantasy of economic stability that appears everywhere in Dickens, a fantasy in which the loss of money clears the way for secure domestic fortune. She celebrates her poverty by offering herself as the dowry that Gay will receive instead of more apparent wealth: "'Oh Walter, if I could have brought you millions, I never could have been so happy. . . . I am . . . nothing but your wife.' The light hand stole about his neck" (885).

Florence serves as her lover's necklace here, replacing the money that she gave him on the eve of his departure for Barbados:

> "You remember the last time I saw you, Walter, before you went away?"

He put his hand into his breast, and took out a little purse. "I have always worn it round my neck! If I had gone down in the deep, it would have been with one at the bottom of the sea." (803)

The treasure that Gay keeps in his breast signals a link between concealing and securing treasure, a link that prepares for the identification of these things when the money purse is followed by Florence herself as the form of Gay's fortune: "The woman's heart of Florence, with its undivided treasure, can be yielded only once." Conflating, as it does, exposure to view and the transfer of property, the term "yield" effectively registers capital's aspect in *Dombey and Son*, an aspect from which the "undivided treasure" of Florence is exempted. The woman "lost" to the "flashes" and "uncovering riches" that surround her is Gay's intimate estate—at once an object for his eyes only and a possession securely fastened to him.

The marriage of Gay and Florence is cast as a cure by the novel; it is characterized as the agent and figure of reformation of the loveless pride that afflicts both home and downtown departments of Dombey and Son. Moreover, the marriage secures another kind of reformation, rescuing phallic propriety from a specter of matriarchy that haunts the novel: "A succession of man-traps, stretching out infinitely . . . a series of ages of oppression and coercion" (954). The submissive, sequestered bride replaces Edith Dombey, who "would often . . . go out and come home, treading the round of London life with no more heeding of his liking or disliking, pleasure or displeasure, than if he had been her groom." But the marriage of Florence and Gay more precisely remedies the relation between Captain Cuttle, one of Gay's ineffectual fathers, and the captain's tyrannical landlady.

Mrs. MacStinger's power over Cuttle derives from a property relation. He is a prisoner at Number Nine Briggs Place, because he is only a tenant, rather than the lord of the manor:

> "I beg your pardon, Ma'am," said Florence. . . . "Is this Captain Cuttle's house?"
>
> "No," said Mrs MacStinger.
>
> "Not Number Nine?" asked Florence, hesitating.
>
> "Who said it wasn't Number Nine?" said Mrs MacStinger. . . .
>
> . . . "Perhaps you can have the goodness to tell us where Captain Cuttle lives, Ma'am, as he don't live here."
>
> "Who says he don't live here" retorted the implacable MacStinger. "I said it wasn't Cap'en Cuttle's house—and it ain't his house—and forbid

it, that it ever should be his house—for Cap'en Cuttle don't know how to keep a house—and don't deserve to have a house—it's *my* house—and when I let the upper floor to Cap'en Cuttle, oh I do a thankless thing, and cast pearls before swine." (404)

The landlady's harassment gains material force when she throws a fence at her door to prevent free entry to Cuttle's chamber: she incessantly interferes with others' access to him, and this interference is specifically the assertion of her property right. Constantly cleaning house, Mac-Stinger exercises her proprietary prerogative by exiling Cuttle to "a very small desolate island, lying about midway in an ocean of soap and water." The proprietress refuses to allow others to *see* the Captain, generating endless "artificial fog" with her "washing" that does nothing in the novel but obscure Cuttle. And while ownership and concealment are only metonymically allied at Number Nine Briggs Place during the day, at night they are condensed by the hapless captain's dream work: "He dreamed that old Sol Gills was married to Mrs MacStinger, and kept by that lady in a secret chamber on a short allowance of victuals" (789). In this nightmare vision, the landlady keeps what she conceals and conceals what she keeps.

The sheltered domestic estate in *Dombey and Son* that evades the alienating floodlights of capital and, along the way, corrects the narrative's matriarchal swerve is crucially entailed: Florence can be held in secret only if she is held innocently. This stipulation first appears in the novel's repeated characterizations of a gruff sailor's chaste treatment of "the sweet creetur grow'd a woman" (760) when they are alone together. Exiled from her father's house, Florence seeks shelter at the midshipman's shop, and the only person she finds there is Captain Cuttle, with whom she remains for some time, unchaperoned: "'Oh Captain Cuttle!' cried Florence, putting her hands together, and speaking wildly. 'Save me! Keep me here! Let no one know where I am!'" With anxious repetitiveness, the novel announces over and over again the captain's great "respect" (760) for Florence: "Captain Cuttle was so respectful of her, and had such a reverence for her, in this new character, that he would not have held in his arms, while she was unconscious, for a thousand pounds" (760). "Impressed by the possession of his tremendous secret," Cuttle conducts himself with "the chivalry of any old knight-errant" (765): "There was an entire change in the Captain's face . . . the kind of gravity that sat upon his features was quite new to them, and was as great an improvement to them as if they had undergone some sublimating process" (769). Florence is as "safe" alone with Cuttle at the midshipman's shop as she would be "at the top of St Paul's Cathedral, with the ladder cast off."

His fear that he cannot sustain this "sublimating process" makes Walter Gay anxious about sequestering her at the midshipman's shop when he returns from his West Indian exploit to find her there: "'She ought not to be alone here; ought she, Captain Cuttle?' said Walter anxiously." Gay's anxiety results from his discovery that the child he left behind has become a "woman," a maturation that in *Dombey and Son* is specifically defined as a matter of sexualization, as Edith's complaint against her mother reveals: "What childhood did you ever leave me? I was [always] a woman—artful, designing . . . laying snares for men" (472).

The stipulation I am describing helps us to understand Gay as he explains to Florence that he cannot sustain their intimacy in private:

> "If you had been . . . surrounded as you should be by loving and admiring friends . . . and if you had called me brother, then, in your affectionate remembrance of the past, I could have answered to the name from my distant place, with no inward assurance that I wronged your spotless truth by doing so. But here—and now!"
>
> "Oh thank you, thank you Walter! Forgive my having wronged you so much. I had no one to advise me. I am quite alone." (805)

At first glance, we are struck by the incoherence of this passage: since Walter's point is that his feelings for the woman are different from his feelings for the girl, and therefore that it would be wrong for him to assume the innocent role of Florence's brother, what would grant him the "inward assurance" that he wouldn't wrong her "spotless truth" even if she *were* surrounded by friends? But in keeping with the rule of privacy I am describing here, Gay's sexual desire for Florence is marked as a violation only when he is alone with her.

In *The Policing of Families*, Jacques Donzelot locates a social contract whose developments and redefinitions help constitute the history of the modern family, a contract according to which the family's autonomy is tolerated in exchange for its conformity to and reproduction of social norms, especially the regulation of sexual desire and behavior.[14] While the midshipman's shop doesn't contain an immediate family, the group that it does house functions like one, and I want to suggest that a version of the contract that Donzelot isolates is at work here. An ambitious policeman addresses a vague warning to the midshipman's shop when

Florence and Cuttle are there alone, a warning that furnishes a figure for this contract:

> The beadle of that quarter, a man of an ambitious character . . . went so far as to say to an opposite neighbour, that . . . [Cuttle] had better not try it on there—without more particularly mentioning what—and further, that he, the Beadle, would keep his eye upon him. (790)

The privacy of the domestic unit sheltered by the shutters of the midshipman's shop depends upon the chastity of its inhabitants.

We can notice this contract at work both in the chaste "image" of Florence that Gay "preserve[s] in his mind" and in the chaste "child" he later "encircles" as his wife. As he prepares for his departure for Barbados, Gay "pledged himself to cherish and protect her very image, in his banishment, with brotherly regard; to garner up her simple faith, inviolate; and hold himself degraded if he breathed upon it any thought that was not in her own breast when she gave it to him"; rejecting the "libelous" imagination of her as "a woman," Gay "could do no better than preserve her image in his mind . . . restraining him like an angel's hand from anything unworthy." Later, when Gay and Florence are engaged, she ceases to be a "woman" that must be "repulsed," and merges with the image of innocence that he "cherishes and protects": "a hushed child." The frozen memory of Florence lodged in his mind and the figure of the child engirded by the proprietary right called marriage ("a right above all others to defend and guard you") are the same thing, the private estate of innocence.

This image of innocence sequestered within the private borders of the midshipman's shop, of Walter Gay's mind, and of matrimony is also an imperative that *prescribes* innocence: if purification depends on privatization (only when things are pure are they allowed to be private), the opposite is also true. Privatization is cast by the novel as the means of sustaining or producing purity: Florence seeks shelter at the midshipman's shop to erase the mark of sexuality that her father branded on her; Gay preserves Florence's image in his mind, which is at once to maintain it within confines where it is unavailable to the apprehension of others and to arrest its sexualizing maturation; his marriage to Florence is a chastity belt, an engirding contract, a "precious trust" to "defend and guard" her "spotless truth."

Privacy is the means of purity, and purity is the means of privacy. The exchange between Gay and Florence that results in their engagement suggests as much: "'I left a child. I find a woman.' The colour overspread her face. She made a gesture as if of entreaty that he would say no more, and her face dropped upon her hands"(804). Florence no longer needs to cover herself at the end of the passage:

Blessed Sunday Bells, ringing so tranquilly in their entranced and happy ears! Blessed Sunday peace and quiet harmonising with the calmness in their souls, and making holy air around them! Blessed twilight stealing on, and shading her so soothingly and gravely, as she falls asleep, like a hushed child, upon the bosom she has clung to. (806)

Not even the twilight that shades Florence in this quiet scene is necessary to render her covert. She is a "hushed child": her concealment is a constituent of her innocent character.

The capacity of chastity to produce privacy appears most strikingly in a passage where the reader joins the "hungry gazers" outside the midshipman's shop, who are frustrated in their efforts to see through its shutters:

Clinging to this rough creature as the last asylum of her bleeding heart, she laid her head upon his honest shoulder, and clasped him round his neck, and would have kneeled down to bless him, but that he divined her purpose, and held her up like a true man.

"Steady!" said the Captain. "Steady! You're too weak to stand you see, my pretty, and must lie down here again. There, there!" To see the Captain lift her on the sofa, and cover her with his coat, would have been worth a hundred state sights. "And now," said the Captain, "you must take some breakfast, lady lass. . . . And arter that you shall go aloft to old Sol Gill's room, and fall asleep there, like an angel." (762)

The denial of sexuality recorded in this passage is granted a curiously unique privacy. The contrary-to-fact proposition here—"To see the Captain lift her on the sofa, and cover her with his coat, would have been worth a hundred state sights"—indicates that we do not see this scene, but why are we any less able to see this than any other sight that the novel describes? Here the relation between tool and goal that I described earlier is reversed: covering a potentially sexual object is the means for producing inscrutability rather than the other way around. Chastity is the condition of privacy, both because it sanctions privacy and because it generates it.

In contrast, Florence's characterization as "woman" brings an access of color and an effort to conceal: if innocence is the condition of privacy in *Dombey and Son*, sexuality is a condition of its cancellation. In his dispute with the "repressive hypothesis," Michel Foucault identifies sexuality as a target and alibi for surveillance, rather than simply a repressed object: "What is peculiar to modern societies . . . is not that they consigned sex to a shadow existence, but that they dedicated themselves to speaking of it *ad infinitum*, while exploiting it as *the* secret." Foucault argues that sexuality is constituted as a secret that cannot be maintained by being cast as a form of display: "Sex had to be put into words." Sexuality in modern societies becomes a secret that cannot be kept, because it becomes "something to say. . . . Whether in the form of a subtle confession in confidence or an authoritarian interrogation, sex—be it refined or rustic—had to be put into words."[15] As the drift of this remark suggests, sexuality is not simply an object observed, according to Foucault's account, but a subject that displays by its very nature; sexuality is not a substance, but a sign, a means of appearance.

Dombey and Son registers the aspect of sexuality that Foucault describes here, casting it with capital as something inherently indiscreet. Edith's erotic emanations make this clear to us. The "base and wretched aim of every . . . display" that Edith "learnt" was the "artful . . . laying [of] snares for men" (472–73). Edith's "beauty," that which "calls forth admiration" (367) from "all kinds of men" (473), is "a badge or livery she hated" (466). The constant defeat of her reserve ("it was a remarkable characteristic of this lady's beauty that it appeared to vaunt and assert itself without her aid, and against her will") resembles Carker's unspoken sycophantry, as quiet as a loudspeaker:

> "Mr Dombey, to a man in your position from a man in mine, there is no show of subservience . . . that I should think sufficient." If he had carried these words about with him, printed on a placard . . . he could not have been more explicit than he was. (239)

The shows and signs (the "displays", the "badge," and the "livery") that work through the figure of Edith to tempt men are like the landscape that adorns Carker's yard: "The lawn, the soft, smooth slope, the flower garden, the clumps of trees where graceful forms of ash and willow are not wanting . . . bespeak an amount of elegant comfort within" (553). The rumor of an erotic body lying in the shape of the "soft smooth slope" and "graceful forms" of this passage again designates sexuality as a kind of display, or a form of address.

Moreover, sexuality, like capital, is nothing in *Dombey and Son* but a form of exhibition. Like the "credit" that constitutes the "resources" of the house, the "elegant comfort" signaled by these sexual shapes, the "rich colours, excellently blended," that "meet the eye at every turn," "the furniture—its proportions admirably devised to suit the shapes and sizes of the small rooms," and the "few choice prints and pictures" are themselves "one voluptuous cast—mere shows of form and colour" (554).

Sexuality achieves the same circulation as capital. This achievement appears in the prostitute's narrative, which takes place in chapter 34: "I am a woman—not a girl, now—and you and I needn't make a show of our history, like the men in Court" (571). Alice Marwood need not make a show because she is a show: "Lost and degraded as she was, there was a beauty in her, both of face and form which, even in its worst expression, could not but be recognized as such by anyone regarding her with the least attention" (571–72). The availability of Marwood's beauty to even the most casual observer, like the "badge or livery" that Edith is compelled to wear, suggests the absolutely public character of the show of sexuality. This character confirms itself when the history of the prostitute's corruption, like the capital of the house's name, merges with the novel. Upon her return from exile, Marwood narrates her story to her mother:

> Listen, mother, to a word or two. If we understand each other now, we shall not fall out any more, perhaps. I went away a girl, and have come back a woman. I went away undutiful enough, and have come back no better, you may swear. But have you been very dutiful to me? (570)

After this, Marwood's story takes a backward turn, and instead of telling her mother about her experience in exile, she narrates the events of her fall into prostitution. This is curious, since she surely knows that her ostensible auditor already knows this part of her history. As Marwood's story progresses, its putative audience recedes, and its real recipient emerges into view—not her mother, but rather the reader of the novel:

> There was a child called Alice Marwood . . . born, among poverty and neglect, and nursed in it. . . . She lived in homes like this, and in the streets, with a crowd of little wretches like herself; and yet she brought good looks out of this childhood. So much the worse for her. She had better have been hunted and worried to death for ugliness. . . . There was a girl called Alice Marwood. She was handsome. She was taught too late, and taught all wrong. She was too well cared for, too well trained, too well helped on, too much looked after. . . . What came to that girl comes to thousands each year. It was only ruin, and she was born to it. (571)

Like the identification of the capital of the house's name as a "History," the prostitute joins the third-person voice of the novel; like the story of capital, the sexual narrative in *Dombey and Son* achieves the utmost extent of publicity available to it, the boundary of the text in which it is situated.[16]

The intimacy between sexuality and capital surpasses the terms of analogy in *Dombey and Son*: in various ways, the novel charts the merging of these forms of exhibition. Capital's sexualization and sexuality's capitalization together compose the spectacle of Edith, "offered" on the "market" at once as a commodity, "appraised, hawked and vended," and as an erotic entity, "the bye-word of all kinds of men" (473). The interconvertibility of these modes of publicity appears in the "clashing of voices" that is the warfare between Dombey and Edith. If capital recruits sexuality to perform its pageantries, if the House of Dombey purchases Edith's "beauty" as a form of "reflecting credit," capital, in turn, falls into the form of sexuality. Edith's dressing room completes the capitalist's subservience to its "haughty mistress," "as if he had been her groom," by casting the exhibitions of wealth as sexual passion:

> He glanced round the room: saw how . . . the luxuries . . . were scattered here and there, and disregarded . . . in a steadfast haughty disregard of costly things . . . he saw riches . . . made of no account. The very diamonds . . . that rose and fell impatiently upon her bosom, seemed to pant to break the chain that clasped them round her neck, and roll down on the floor where she might tread upon them. (651)

Routed and retreating, the financier casts a backward glance, which again apprehends the display of wealth in the shape of the display of beauty:

> [Dombey] looked back, as he went out at the door, upon the well-lighted and luxurious room, the beautiful and glittering objects everywhere displayed, the shape of Edith in its rich dress seated before her glass, and the face of Edith as the glass presented it to him. (657)

The eroticization of capital that takes place in Edith's dressing room appears again when Carker apprehends the financial transactions of the firm in the shape of a body "laid bare before him" (722), and again when, through a curious construction that catches wealth in the act of disrobing, commodities appear to the gaze of consumers in the same shape: "Riches are uncovering in shops" (902).

My final task in this section is to notice the genesis of Gay's intimate franchise, to trace the path of privatization, the process of desexualization and decapitalization, that makes way for his domestic estate. The innocent, intimate entity that Gay preserves in his mind and encircles in his arm is founded on the extinction of a sexualized, commodified version of Florence—a story, a widely available "adventure," in which the boy takes a "delightful interest":

> That spice of romance and love of the marvelous, of which there was a pretty strong infusion in the nature of young Walter Gay . . . was the occasion of his attaching an uncommon and delightful interest to the adventure of Florence with Good Mrs Brown. He pampered and cherished it in his memory, especially that part of it with which he had been associated; until it became the spoiled child of his fancy, and took its own way, and did what it liked with it.
>
> The recollection of those incidents, and his own share in them, may have been made the more captivating, perhaps, by the weekly dreamings of old Sol and Captain Cuttle . . . the latter gentleman had even gone so far as to purchase a ballad . . . that had long fluttered among many others . . . on a dead wall in the Commercial Road: which poetical performance set forth the courtship and nuptials of a promising young coal-whipper with a certain "lovely Peg," the accomplished daughter of the master and part owner of a Newcastle collier. In this stirring legend, Captain Cuttle descried a profound metaphysical bearing on the case of Walter and Florence; and it excited him so much, that on very festive occasions . . . he would roar through the whole song in the little back parlour; making an amazing shake on the word Pe-e-eg, with which every verse concluded, in compliment to the heroine of the piece. (172)

The "captivating" "adventure of Florence with Good Mrs Brown" is the center of a general atmosphere of sexual excitation that culminates with Cuttle's "amazing shake." Our sense of the sexual character of this adventure is supported by its figuration as the "spoiled child of his fancy" who "did what it liked with it," a spoiled child like Alice Marwood or Edith Dombey. The sexuality of this adventure also suggests itself in the source of Gay's interest in them, the "spice of romance and the love of the marvelous" instilled in him by his uncle, a "secret attraction" toward "books" and "stories" that "lure" and "charm" (96).

As the economic language that describes Gay's relation to it suggests, this erotic fantasy merges with the commodity to which it is attached. Their radical identification is registered by the passage when it casts the commodity that Cuttle purchases on Commercial Road as an agent of eroticization; the rehearsal of the ballad of "lovely Peg" makes, or would make, the adventure of Florence and Good Mrs Brown more "captivating." The fusion of these two modes of publicity is furthered by the following paragraph, which seeks to negate, at once, the suspicion that Gay's interest in the adventures of Florence is sexual and the suspicion that it is mercenary: "The sentiment of all this was as boyish and innocent as could be" (173).

And, in keeping with the publicizing character of capital and sexuality, this eroticized, commodified "adventure of Florence with Good Mrs Brown" is widely available. The similarity between Walter Gay and the young coal whipper is the distance between these boys and the girls in whom they take "interest": Gay is a lowly employee of Dombey and Son, as removed from Florence as the coal whipper is from lovely Peg. But just as the gap between Peg and her proletariat paramour is closed *within* the ballad, the gap between Walter Gay and the eroticized, capitalized figure of *his* master's daughter is closed *by* the "adventure," a form of publication in which even the otherwise unenfranchised can take "interest."

As the boy grows, his capitalized and erotic fantasies of the girl give way to the chaste conception of Florence that he keeps to himself. The sexualized, capitalized adventure is surpassed and replaced by the intimate entity we have examined, the "indefinite image" of innocence: "He could do no better than preserve her image . . . precious . . . unchangeable, and indefinite in all but its power of giving him pleasure, and restraining him like an angel's hand from anything unworthy" (288). This "indefinite" image of Florence is privatized to the same extent that the covered girl is in the midshipman's shop when Cuttle shelters her from the gaze of "hungry spectators" within and beyond the bounds of the novel. We have no access at all to this angelic, "indefinite" sight; like the view offered by the fortress walls of an estate, a view that only serves to confirm the viewer's exclusion from the sight, our conception of Gay's image is restricted to the recognition that it is harbored by and directed to Gay. In contrast to the obscurity of this "image," the "exciting" "romantic" fantasies that precede this private image are described in great detail:

> They set off Florence very much, to his fancy. . . . Sometimes he
> thought (and then he walked very fast) what a grand thing it would
> have been for him to have been going to sea on the day after that first

meeting, and to have gone, and to have done wonders there, and to have stopped away a long time, and to have come back an Admiral of all the colours of the dolphin, or at least a Post-Captain . . . and have married Florence (then a beautiful young woman) in spite of Mr Dombey's teeth, cravat, and watch chain, and borne her away to the blue shores of somewhere or other, triumphantly. (173–74)

This fantasy is as available to us as it is to Gay, and this mutual accessibility corresponds to the fact that the "adventure of Florence with Good Mrs Brown" is as available to Gay as it is to us, since this adventure takes place first as an episode within the narrative of the novel itself (chapter 6). The chaste figure of Florence is taken from the edge of the novel where she is situated when, with lovely Peg, she is cast in the publicizing shape of capital and sexuality.

3

I want now to situate the novel's establishment of secure, secret property in its global context. Like the Indian fabrics that adorn the houses of Victorian novels, the dry dream and the white bride that Walter Gay "garners up" within the private confines of domestic estate involve a dark foreign relation. The recession of the capitalized, sexualized "adventure" that precedes Gay's private treasure of chastity, the passing away that enables the covert possession that follows, depends upon the Orientalization of the boy's early fortunes.

Before I proceed to consider how Gay's erotic adventures are Orientalized, and how this Orientalization enables their termination, I need first to define and survey the Oriental presence in Dickens's writings. For "Oriental," I rely on Edward Said's designation of the broadest meaning of the term, "the demarcation between East and West," and refer to a heterogeneous cluster of ideas about regions and cultures that are now sometimes called collectively the Third World.[17] It is my aim throughout this section to justify the use of this comprehensive term by isolating common features that draw together Dickens's various accounts of the non-western, accounts ranging from recognizably fanciful versions of the Orient—the colorful affluence and affluence of color that inhabit the "rich East India House," or "that gorgeous storehouse of Eastern Riches," as Dickens calls the Arabian Nights—to pseudo-ethnographic descriptions of Dark Continents, populated by squalid savages.[18]

Mrs. Jellyby's reverse myopia in *Bleak House*—"[her] eyes . . . had a curious habit of seeming to look a long way off . . . [a]s if . . . they could see nothing nearer than Africa!" (36)—may speak poorly for her capacity as domestic monitor, but it speaks well for the drawing power of the African spectacle. The distant object of the philanthropist's fascination describes generally the geography of the Oriental in Dickens's work, where the East is always an exhibition.

Things Oriental join the gallery of capital and sexuality in *Dombey and Son*; their exotic hues are spectacular:

> The rich East India House, teeming with suggestions of precious stuffs and stones, tigers, elephants, howdahs, hookahs, umbrellas, palm trees, palanquins, and gorgeous princes of a brown complexion sitting on carpets, with their slippers very much turned up at the toes. (87)

The wealth displayed by the East India House is a wealth of display, composed of curious objects and fabulous colors that invite the gaze. Just as Mrs. Jellyby sees the distant Niger with utter lucidity, this passage vividly perceives even the "suggestion" of the spectacular Orient: the mere intimation of the catalog of Indian objects teems with "gorgeous" light that extends to illuminate the surrounding landscape. Immediately before its appearance is the novel's account of the close and encrypted centers of wealth: "The Royal Exchange was close at hand; the Bank of England, with its vaults of gold and silver 'down among the dead men' underground was their magnificent neighbour." This darkness is interrupted by the East India House, and then "anywhere in the immediate vicinity there might be seen pictures of ships speeding away full sail to all parts of the world; outfitting warehouses ready to pack off anybody anywhere" (87–88). With the intervention of "gorgeous" Oriental color, there dawns a visibility that replaces the closeness that precedes it; the darkness of crypts gives way to the gallery of global expansion.

Like capital and sexuality, the Oriental, for Dickens, displays by its nature. The tigers and elephants that take part in the spectacle of the East India House help us think of this catalog of curious sights as a kind of parade, like the one that the opium addict witnesses at the beginning of *The Mystery of Edwin Drood*:

> The Sultan goes by to his palace in long procession. Ten thousand scimitars flash in the sunlight, and thrice ten thousand dancing girls strew flowers. Then follow white elephants caparisoned in countless gorgeous colours. (1)

And the Indian or Arabian parade is matched by the African theater described by Dickens in an essay entitled "The Noble Savage" (1851).[19] The savage is always "exhibited" in England, sometimes in "a picturesque and glowing book," sometimes "in an elegant theatre, fitted with appropriate scenery." More strikingly, the savage is pictured by Dickens as a figure for a landscape, or a player for a stage even in his natural habitat. The African is not only the object of Occidental surveillance, according to Dickens's account; that is, like sexuality and capital, the savage is not only an object scrutinized, but also a character whose native aspect is an exhibition:

> The women being at work in the fields, hoeing the Indian corn, and the noble savage being asleep in the shade, the chief has sometimes the condescension to come forth and lighten the labour by looking at it. On these occasions he seats himself in his own savage chair, and is attended by his shield-bearer: who holds over his head a shield of cowhide—in shape like an immense muscle shell—fearfully and wonderfully, after the manner of a theatrical supernumerary.

This passage casts both the fields of labor at which the noble savage directs his gaze and the savage spectator himself, adorned by stage scenery and "a theatrical supernumerary," as the object of exhibition: the landscape of the Oriental is comprehended by the frame of the picture or the space of the stage.

The noble savage lightens the site of toil by looking at it, and this suggests what is true about the Oriental landscape generally: it is a sight shaped by its apprehension. Like the other forms of publication that I have examined, the Oriental cannot be separated from its appearance; its purely spectacular character is suggested by its frequent shape as hallucination—the "arabesques" and "miniature 'tigers and lions'" that only Paul Dombey discerns in the "paperhanging in the house" (234) or the opium-induced visions entertained in *The Mystery of Edwin Drood*.

Like money, the Orient makes a spectacle of power and glory for the eyes of all men. Oriental publication is capable of achieving the extent attained by capital and sexuality—the spectacle of the sultan that commences *The Mystery of Edwin Drood* disconcerts us because it is unframed by any containing narrative and is instead, like Alice Marwood's story, coincident with the boundary of the book itself. But there is a decisive difference between the Oriental exhibition and those that take place under, or better, as, the sign of capital and sexuality. *Drood*'s Oriental parade features the sultan himself at its center; the riches of the East

India House culminate with "gorgeous princes of a brown complexion sitting on carpets, with their slippers very much turned up at their toes"; other Oriental displays in the novel include a "fierce idol with a mouth from ear to ear, and a murderous visage" (330), "two exhausted negroes holding up two withered branches of candelabra on the sideboard" (509) and a barber's waxen effigy, "bald as a Musselman"; unlike the displays of sexuality and capital, Oriental exhibition is always incarnated.

Such exhibition is thus unlike those of capital and sexuality, whose detachability from the body renders them similar to the oracular voice of Bunsby, Captain Cuttle's laconic prophet, "[a] deep, gruff, husky utterance, which seemed to have no connexion with Bunsby, and certainly had not the least effect on his face." Money's status as "spirit" manifests the metaphysical nature that characterizes capital, generally, in the novel. Dombey's identification with another sign of capital is affiliated with the apotheosis of Christ:

> A.D. had no concern with anno Domini, but stood for anno Dombei—and Son. He had risen, as his father had before him, in the course of life and death, from Son to Dombey, and for nearly twenty years had been the sole representative of the Firm. (50)

To be the representative of the firm is to be he who rises after a course of life and death; to be the sole representative of the firm is to be the firm's soul representative. The hint offered by this passage, that Dombey leaves the body behind to become the representative of the firm, appears again in the novel's dark description of the son's christening, the solemn ceremony in which he assumes the name of the house. Paul Dombey's interpellation as this sign of capital merges with his funeral:

> "Please to bring the child in quick out of the air there," whispered the beadle, holding open the inner door of the church. Little Paul might have asked with Hamlet, "into my grave?" so chill and earthy was the place. . . . Then the clergyman . . . appeared like the principal character in a ghost story, "a tall figure all in white;" at sight of whom Paul rent the air with his cries, and never left off again till he was taken out black in the face. (114)

Dombey and Son's anticipation of Paul's assumption of the position of son of the firm as his "after-life" again affirms the notion that the capital of the house's name appears after death. Here is Dombey, predicting his son's placement as the "Son." "He will make what powerful friends he pleases in after-life when he is actively maintaining—and extending, if that is possible—the dignity and credit of the Firm" (103).

These accounts of the career of Dombey and Son as characters that take place in "after-life," these depictions of capital as ghosts or epitaphs (someone in the novel aptly notices the difficulty in distinguishing the family from tombstones), dramatize the discrepancy between the displays of capital and the fleshly body. This distinction is registered in different terms, in the passage we considered earlier, where the "Son of the Firm" is made the subject of a novel:

> [Dombey] loved his son with all the love he had. If there were a warm place in his frosty heart, his son occupied it; if its very hard surface could receive the impression of any image, the image of that son was there; though not so much as an infant, or as a boy, but as a grown man—the "Son" of the Firm. (151)

As the quotation marks that surround the "Son" of the firm indicate, the maturation figured here is a kind of textualization that transcends the flesh: the "warm place" that can shelter the body of the son is replaced by a blank slate that can receive the imprint of his image.

The "after-life" of capital shadows, but remains separate from, the fleshly body; the "badge or livery" of sexuality is adjacent to but distinct from it. If the erotic verges or impinges on the bodily form in *Dombey and Son*, it nevertheless falls short of incarnation. The figure insinuated in the landscape of Carker's cottage, in the "uncovering" commodities, or in the spectacle of jewels that "*seems* to pant" (my emphasis) suggests but never becomes a body. Edith's beauty is a costume *attached to* her figure, a "badge or livery she hates." This adjacency is intensified when the body serves as the surface for the text of sexuality; here again, for example, is the novel's account of Edith's confrontation with the fallen woman: "It may have been that she saw *upon* her face some traces which she knew were lingering in her soul, if not yet written *on* that index" (662, my emphases). But while the body serves as its surface or mannequin, it remains separate from the words or clothes of sexual display.

It is the distinction between her sexual beauty and her obdurate body that enables Edith's adamantine resistance to both Dombey and Carker:

> "You see me looking on you now, and you can read the warmth of passion for you that is breathing in my face." Not a curl of the proud lip, not a flash of the dark eye, nothing but the same intent and searching look, accompanied these words. "You know my general history. You have spoken of my mother. Do you think you can degrade, or bend or break *me* to submission and obedience?"[20]

This blankness of the flesh, a bodily reticence quite opposed to the "general history" of her prostitution which makes Edith a "bye-word of all kinds of men" (473), appears again to repel Carker when he seeks from the wife of his master "voluptuous compensation for past restraint" (865): "He sprung up from his chair. . . . She put her hand into her bosom, and not a finger trembled, not a hair upon her head was stirred. He stood still" (858).

If the exhibitions of capital and sexuality are different from the flesh that they work through in *Dombey and Son*, the body itself composes the spectacle that inhabits the dark landscape of Africa, according to "The Noble Savage":

> He sticks a fishbone through his visage, or bits of trees through the lobes of his ears, or birds' feathers in his head . . . he flattens his hair between two boards, or spreads his nose over the breadth of his face, or drags his lower lip down by great weights, or blackens his teeth, or knocks them out, or paints one cheek red and the other blue, or tattoos himself or oils himself, or rubs his body with fat, or crimps it with knives.

While sexuality is a garment or a text that dwells on Edith's body, the savage exhibition penetrates and merges with the savage physique. Savage display is a body show, and Dickens's antipathy toward "the noble stranger" is body hatred:

> Think of the Bushmen. Think of the two men and the two women who have been exhibited about England for some years. Are the majority of persons—who remember the horrid little leader of that party in his festering bundle of hides, with his filth and his antipathy to water, and his straddled legs, and his odious eyes shaded by his brutal hand . . . conscious of an affectionate yearning towards that noble savage, or is it idiosyncratic in me to abhor, detest, abominate, and abjure him? I have no reserve on this subject, and will frankly state that, setting aside that stage of the entertainment when he counterfeited the death of some creature he had shot, by laying his head on his hand, and shaking his left leg—at which time I think it would have been justifiable homicide to slay him—I have never seen that group sleeping, smoking, and expectorating round their brazier, but I have sincerely desired that something might happen to the charcoal smouldering therein, which would cause the immediate suffocation of the whole of the noble strangers.

Dickens's savage is not merely contained in carnality, wrapped in "a festering bundle of hides," but composed of it: "straddled legs," "odious eyes," "brutal hand" "sleeping," "expectorating." The savage most dramatically embodies exhibition when he performs a pantomime: "That stage of the entertainment when he counterfeited the death of some creature he had shot, by laying his head on his hand, and shaking his left leg." Even when the exhibited entity is represented *by* rather than contained *in* the savage's physical form, Dickens dwells on and emphasizes the body that presents it.

It is this bodily persistence that makes "dramatic expression" impossible for the "Noble Savage."

> There was Mr. Catlin, some few years ago . . . who had lived among more tribes of Indians than I need reckon up here, and who had written a picturesque and glowing book about them. With his party of Indians squatting and spitting on the table before him, or dancing their miserable jig . . . he called, in all good faith, upon his civilized audience to take notice of their symmetry and grace and perfect limbs, and the exquisite expression of their pantomime. . . . Whereas, as mere animals they were wretched creatures very low in the scale and very poorly formed; and as men and women possessing any power of truth or dramatic expression by means of action, they were no better than the chorus of an Italian Opera in England—and would have been worse if such a thing were possible.

The attribution of abstract values ("symmetry," "grace") to the physical shape of the noble savage is given the lie by his actual body—"spitting," "squatting," "poorly formed," just as abstract expression produced *by means* of dramatic action is outside his strictly carnal capacity.

When the spectacle of capital or sexuality is figured as text, it is separated from the body; in contrast, the language of the savage is always incarnated. This embodiment, suggested by the subject of his poetry— "O what a delightful chief [we have]! O what a delicious quantity of blood he sheds! O how he tears the flesh of his enemies and crunches the bones!"—is dramatized by a ceremony that stars his poet laureate: "This literary gentleman wears a leopard's head over his own, and a dress of tigers' tails; he has the appearance of having come express on his hind legs from the Zoological Gardens." While Edith's is a "low plain voice, that neither rose or fell," a nearly abstract voice, whose only physical feature is its absence of feature, the noble savage is always "howling, whistling, stamping, raving"; the bodily tenor of his voice is ever obtrusive.

Dickens conveys his conception of the bodily character of the exhibitions of the noble savage most effectively at one point in the essay, when he pictures the African engaged in an act of violence:

Every gentleman who finds himself excited by the subject, instead of crying "Hear, hear!," as is the custom with us, darts from the rank and tramples out the life, or crushes the skull, or mashes the face, or scoops out the eyes, or breaks the limbs, or performs a whirlwind of atrocities on the body, of an imaginary enemy.

Our realization that the savage performs a pantomime here is delayed until the final phrase of this sentence, a delay that is extended by the comma that precedes that phrase, and by then it is too late to dispel the effect created by the lurid detail that precedes it: the bare indication of the "imaginary" character of the violence performed by the savage does little to remove our sense of its physical form and force. Here, Dickens coaxes us to share his own obsession with the African's spectacular body.

Dickens grants some approval to the "modesty" of one "exemplary" exhibition of the savage, but this modesty is mitigated by the savage's smell: "They are rather picturesque to the eye, though far from odoriferous to the nose." If, as Marx declares in a gleeful allusion to the punch line of a story about the abstractness of money, *pecunia non olet*, the exhibition of savages *always* smells according to Dickens; the taint of the body never departs the frame of the Oriental spectacle.

Dickens's insistence on the bodily character of Oriental exhibition is most noticeably registered when it is superimposed on versions of Oriental spectacle that were previously identified with the transcendence of the body. In *Dombey and Son*, the decline of Cleopatra's flesh is underwritten by her decline *into* flesh: This "wrinkled" and "haggard" impersonation of the queen of the Nile "certainly [does] not resembl[e] Shakespeare's Cleopatra, whom age could not wither" (367).

The bodily limits that contain a "shrunken" (657) Cleopatra also foil an Oriental effort to manifest spirit:

Ideas, like ghosts (according to the common notion of ghosts) must be spoken to a little before they will explain themselves; and Toots had long left off asking any questions of his own mind. Some mist there may have been, issuing from that leaden casket, his cranium, which, if it could have taken shape and form, would have become a genie: but it could not; and it only so far followed the example of the smoke in the Arabian story, as to roll out in a thick cloud, and there hang and hover. (234)

In the difference between the "genie," leagued with ideas and ghosts, and the mist that fails to achieve its metaphysical condition, hovering instead around the container of the body, the novel measures again the *restriction* of Oriental spectacle to the boundaries of the physical.

Cleopatra constitutes *Dombey and Son*'s most extended treatment of an Oriental figure, and while I will consider her status as sexual temptress in a moment, I want first to consider her as an instance of Oriental embodiment. The painted face of the savage has its counterpart in Cleopatra's body, which consists of paint: "The wrinkled face . . . with the patched colour on it." Cleopatra "smooths the rosy hue upon her cheeks" and refuses to allow the major to kiss them, "in apprehension of some danger to their bloom." "Such is the figure, painted and patched for the sun to mock, that is drawn slowly through the crowds from day to day" (673).

Again, paint not only dwells on the surface of the Oriental body, it also penetrates it: "She was soon able to sit up . . . to have a little artificial bloom dropped into the hollow of her cheeks." "Arranged as Cleopatra," the entire Oriental body is directed and defined by the work of exhibition: "slightly settling her false curls and false eyebrows with her fan, and showing her false teeth, set off by her false complexion" (361–62). Her languishing body is situated on the deathbed once occupied by Paul Dombey in order to make a spectacle: "The figure . . . substituted for the patient boy's on the same theatre, once more to connect it . . . with decay and death is stretched there" (671–72). The verb that describes Cleopatra's arrangement here characterizes this body as a kind of canvas, a figure "painted and patched for the sun to mock, . . . drawn slowly through the crowds." Cleopatra is not only a body painted, but a body consisting of paint, a drawn figure. *Dombey and Son* most thoroughly describes the radical involvement of the Oriental body in the work of exhibition when, in its first account of Cleopatra, it casts her as a kind of mobile tableau vivant:

> Her attitude in the wheeled chair (which she never varied) was one in which she had been taken in a barouche, some fifty years before, by a then fashionable artist who had appended to his published sketch the name of Cleopatra: in consequence of a discovery made by the critics of the time, that it bore an exact resemblance to that Princess as she reclined on board her galley. . . . The beauty and the barouche had both passed away, but she still preserved the attitude, and for this reason expressly, maintained the wheeled chair and the butting page: there being nothing whatever, except the attitude, to prevent her from walking. (362)

The Oriental character of the incarnation of exhibition manifests itself most curiously in the surreal spectacle created in the eyes of a dark servant, the consequence of the merging of his master's appetite for social exhibition with his appetite for victuals:

> The Major took charge of the whole conversation, and showed as great an appetite in that respect as in regard of the various dainties on the table, among which he may be almost said to have wallowed: greatly to the aggravation of his inflammatory tendencies. . . . When he got [home] . . . his whole form . . . dilated beyond all former experience; and presented to the dark man's view, nothing but a heaving mass of indigo. (192)

When exhibition is embodied, it is also Orientalized.

Such embodiments partake of a commonplace conception of the pure carnality of nonwhite people. They are also involved with what Christine Bolt calls the "hardening of race thinking" that takes place in the mid-Victorian period, the various ideological practices that surround the consolidation of the definition of "race" as a physical category.[21] Bolt describes a crucial instance of this "hardening" in the activities of James Hunt, whose group seceded from the Ethnological Society and founded a rival organization because of its opposition to the proposition of racial equality: "Rejecting the Enlightenment stress on the similarity of men's bodies, the new society's president, Dr James Hunt, and his followers endeavored . . . to prove the inferiority of blacks by means of craniology and comparative anatomy."[22] While the conviction that physical differences among disparate ethnicities are significant is, of course, by no means new in the nineteenth century, it gains intensity during this period. Scientific programs of racial differences that developed in conjunction with evolutionary theory both relied upon and helped reproduce the conception of the body as a sign, as itself a form of display. Moreover, as Hunt's activities suggest, this conception concentrates on the Oriental physique and thus works to concentrate the conception of the body as show on the spectacle of this body.

The shows of capital and sexuality in and beyond *Dombey and Son* are detached from the body; instances or inhabitants of the soul, they are exempted from the accidents of the flesh. In contrast, embodied Oriental exhibition is fastened to a dying animal, subject to the susceptibilities and boundaries of the body. "Certainly not resembling Shakespeare's Cleopatra, whom age could not wither" (367), Dickens's version of the queen of the Nile is not so much a tableau vivant as a *tableau mourant*,

whose decay and death are everywhere defined as the collapse and conclusion of the spectacle with which her body is radically identified. In
her twilight, "the eastern star" is like the "exhausted negroes" who hold
up the "withered candelabra" in her house, a decaying display, "a
patched and pealing" exhibition, "drawn" "for the sun to mock." Cleopatra's collapse into a "cadaver" is everywhere defined as the collapse
of "show": "Mrs Skewton . . . smirk[s] at her cadaverous self in the
glass" and then "suffers her maid to prepare her for repose, tumbling
into ruins like a house of painted cards" (513).

That Cleopatra's demise is the bodily demise of exhibition is revealed
most luridly in the ritual by which she is made ready for night:

> [Her] maid appeared, according to custom, to prepare her gradually for
> night. At night, she should have been a skeleton, with dart and hour-
> glass, rather than a woman, this attendant; for her touch was as the
> touch of Death. The painted object shrivelled underneath her hand; the
> form collapsed, the hair dropped off, the arched dark eyebrows changed
> to scanty tufts of grey; the pale lips shrunk, the skin became cadaverous
> and loose; an old worn, yellow, nodding woman, with red eyes, alone
> remained in Cleopatra's place, huddled up, like a slovenly bundle, in a
> greasy flannel gown. (472)

Cleopatra's "shrivelling" leaves a residue of "ashes" (475): "The maid
who should have been a skeleton . . . collected the ashes of Cleopatra,
and carried them away . . . ready for tomorrow's revivification" (475).
The flames that shrivel Cleopatra are stage fire that encircles both player
and theater, causing at once the demise of a body and a spectacle: the
death of "the Serpent of the Nile" is the "collapse" of form, the "shrivelling" of the "painted object." Cleopatra's death here confirms the
identity that Dickens sets forth earlier in *Dombey and Son*, the identity of
her life with show: "[Cleopatra] never cast off [her affectation] or was it
likely she ever would or could in any place than in the grave" (449). The
"slovenly bundle" that emerges from the fire that murders the dark
queen bears no resemblance to Cleopatra; the "old, worn, yellow, nod-
ding woman, with red eyes" is only the residue of the destruction of the
spectacular Oriental body.

Dombey and Son's account of Cleopatra's nightly demise issues a rumor
that the death of this Oriental exhibition bears with it the death of exhibition per se: "The painted object shrivelled . . . ; the form collapsed."
I mention the synechdochic force suggested in Cleopatra's collapse because it points to the eastern route by which the abstract exhibitions of

capital and sexuality are terminated: through their Orientalization, these things, elsewhere separate from the body, merge with it and are thus subject to bodily death.

The Orientalization of capital arrests the "process of sublimation" by which Dombey and Son become a name, the "course of life and death" that constitutes capital formation in the novel. Consider the exhibition of Dombey's body in "a dark brown room":

> Mr Dombey . . . finding no uncongeniality in . . . the room, in colour a dark brown, with black hatchments of pictures blotching the walls, and twenty-four black chairs, with almost as many nails in them as so many coffins, waiting like mutes on the threshold of the Turkey carpet; and two exhausted negroes holding up two withered branches of candelabra. . . . The owner of the house lived much abroad. . . and the room had gradually put itself into deeper and still deeper mourning for him, until it was become so funereal as to want nothing but a body in it to be quite complete.
>
> No bad representative of the body, for the nonce, in his unbending form, if not in his attitude, Mr Dombey looked down into the cold depths of the dead sea of mahogany. (509–10)

This passage situates the "body" that Dombey represents as the culmination and center of a dark exhibition that begins with the "black hatchments of pictures blotching the walls" and goes on to gain focus as a solemn ceremony. The body, which, as we have seen, is elsewhere in the novel contradistinguished from the garments of spectacle, is here cast as the "complet[ion]" of the costume of mourning that the room "puts itself into." When it dwells in an Oriental region, the body is made the material of display, rather than merely supplying the surface on which display is worn or inscribed.

And the corpse that completes this dark exhibition is the now-embodied form of the abstract display that is capital. In an Oriental theater, the capital of the house's name, the "sole," and by implication, the soul, representative of the firm is cast as flesh. The ghostly representative is Orientalized in a dark brown room, made part of a landscape inhabited and defined by "exhausted negroes" and Turkish carpets, and, in this dusky context, incorporated.

Sexuality is similarly defined by the shape of the body when it is cast under the sign of the Orient. Cleopatra's "mincing" immodesty and "short sleeves," her performance as the Egyptian temptress, enact a parodic version of the commonplace designation of the Oriental as the site of sexuality. And, as the figure of Cleopatra suggests—the figure whose bygone beauty once excited "bucks" to extreme expressions of passion ("bucks threw wine-glasses over their heads by dozens in her honour")— in *Dombey and Son*, this commonplace operates to incarnate the erotic.

Edith's efforts to quarantine the queen of the Nile, to cordon her off from the innocent Florence, manifests this conception of Cleopatra as the incarnation of sexuality:

> "And am I to be told to-night, after all my pains and labour," her mother almost shrieked in her passion, while her palsied head shook like a leaf, "that there is corruption and contagion in me, and that I am not fit company for a girl! What are you, pray? What are you?"
>
> "I have put the question to myself," said Edith, ashy pale, and pointing to the window, "more than once when I have been sitting there, and something in the faded likeness of my sex has wandered past outside; and God knows I have met my reply." (514)

But if Edith acknowledges that she is as much a prostitute as her mother, she does not appear anxious that she herself will infect the temple of purity called Florence. Only the Oriental is the carrier of corruption, only the Oriental is contagious.

The Oriental embodiment of this otherwise abstract exhibition is dispersed throughout *Dombey and Son*, rumored in odd peripheral figurations; it is intimated, for example, in the landscape of Paul Dombey's "arabesque fancies": Paul "found out miniature tigers and lions running up the bedroom walls, and squinting faces *leering* in the squares and diamonds of the floor-cloth" (my emphasis). And, among the "prints and pictures of one voluptuous cast" that festoon Carker's home, "is the figure of a woman, supremely handsome, who, turning away, but with her face addressed to the spectator, flashes her proud glance upon him. . . . Perhaps it is . . . Potiphar's Wife" (554). In the story of this Egyptian temptress, sexuality is decisively located in the body that is covered by clothes, rather than in the clothes themselves: "And it came to pass . . . that his master's wife cast her eyes upon Joseph; and she said, Lie with me. . . . And she caught him by his garment, saying, Lie with me: and he left his garment in her hand, and fled" (Gen. 39:7, 39:12).[23] Edith's body is sexualized only once in the novel, when it is tied to the "slave market": "There is no slave in a market . . . so shown and offered and examined and paraded . . . as I have been," Edith declares, and here she is "submitted to the *license* of look and touch" (my emphasis). In the African or Near Eastern slave market, the body ceases to be the surface of sexuality and becomes its form, the fleshly object of the licentious touch and gaze.[24]

When the representative of the house is cast as a body by the edge of a sea of mahogany, he is cast as a corpse; when sexuality is figured in the frame of an Egyptian temptress, it decays and dies; when the abstract exhibitions of capital and sexuality are Orientalized and thus embodied, they are subject to the limits of the flesh. With this in mind, it is time to return to the scene in *Dombey and Son* where Gay's capitalized, sexualized fantasies disappear in order to notice a kind of Oriental body left behind on the path that leads to the secret site of innocent estate.

The first rumor of the Oriental lineage of these fantasies appears when the novel indicates that they partake of the "spice of romance and love of the marvelous," a spice "of which [Sol Gills] was, in some sort, a distant relation by trade" (96). As Mrs. Perch's ginger preserves suggest, the ginger preserves that the novel stations as a metonym for the West Indies, the spice that Gills's maritime trade brings him into contact with is associated in the nineteenth century with the Orient.

But Gay's "marvelous" adventures are more decisively Orientalized in a faint but crucial figure that underlies these fantasies:

> Walter, so far from forgetting or losing sight of his acquaintance with Florence, only remembered it better and better. As to its adventurous beginning, and all those little circumstances which gave it a distinctive character and relish, he took them into account, more as a pleasant story very agreeable to his imagination . . . than as a part of any matter of fact with which he was concerned. . . . Sometimes he thought . . . what a grand thing it would have been for him to have been going to sea on the day after that first meeting, and to have done wonders there . . . to have come back an Admiral . . . and have married Florence (then a beautiful young woman) . . . and borne her away triumphantly. . . . So it was that he . . . entertained a thousand indistinct and visionary fancies of his own. (173–74)

The boy's daydreams are "a thousand indistinct and visionary fancies" that he "entertains." This phrase alludes to the center of Dickens's fabulous Orient, the locus from which most of its pageantry proceeds in his work, the "entertainment" that he places as a primal scene of storytelling, the Arabian Nights; the Thousand and One Nights, which, as the title page of Edward William Lane's 1838 translation notes, were "Commonly Called, in England, the Arabian Nights' Entertainments."[25] "Everybody is acquainted with that enchanting collection of stories, the

Thousand and One Nights, better known in England as the Arabian Nights' Entertainments," Dickens writes in 1855,[26] and nobody was better acquainted with them than Dickens himself, who, throughout his life, made his writing thick with allusions to "this gorgeous storehouse of Eastern riches."[27]

And these Arabian adventures are terminated in the shape of an insensate body:

> Florence gave him her little hand so freely and so faithfully that Walter held it for some moments in his own, and could not bear to let it go.
>
> Yet Walter did not hold it as he might have held it once, nor did *its touch* awaken those old day-dreams of his boyhood that had floated past him sometimes even lately, and confused him with their broken and indistinct shapes. The purity and innocence of her endearing manner, and its perfect trustfulness, and the undisguised regard for him that lay so deeply seated in her constant eyes, and glowed upon her fair face through the smile that shaded—for alas! it was a smile too sad to brighten—it, were not of their romantic race. They brought back to his thoughts the early deathbed he had seen her tending, and the love the child had borne her; and on the wing of such remembrances she seemed to rise up, far above his idle fancies, into clearer and serener air. (335, my emphasis)

The elegiac atmosphere of this passage derives most apparently from the death of Paul Dombey—Florence's pure manner, her attentive eyes, and her sad smile all recall the death of her brother: "They brought back to his thoughts the early deathbed he had seen her tending." But even before these lines reach the picture of Paul's deathbed, they offer the rumor of a death in the "old day-dreams" that Florence's touch does not "awake[n]." The connection between the death of the boy and the stillness of the "old day-dreams" suggested here extends throughout this passage. Consider the conflation of the "romantic race" of Gay's fantasies with the emissary of solemnity, that which "brought back to [Gay's] thoughts the early deathbed." While the "they" that brings "back to his thoughts the early deathbed" refers to the sadness of the dead boy's sister, this antecedent is confused with the "romantic race" of Gay's adventures, as if the early deathbed accommodated these puerile fabulations.

The confusion of Gay's "thousand indistinct and visionary fancies" with a corpse signals and intensifies a similarity between these things. Like the dead boy, the Arabian adventures are a body: the touch of the hand that cannot awaken Gay's daydreams indicates the fleshly character of their "shape," the bodily character that is the signature of Oriental exhibition in *Dombey and Son*. And the proximity of this body to Paul Dombey's death brings into play a subsidiary meaning of "awake," a meaning that suggests that Florence's touch does not rouse the body, because no touch could. The early deathbed that Florence tends at the end of this paragraph casts its light back on the body that she touches but does not awaken; an elegy for a boy extends to become an elegy for a boy's fantasies.[28]

Thus the extinction of capital and sexuality, the extinction that makes way for private domestic property in *Dombey and Son*, takes shape as the death of an Oriental incarnation. Like the corpse of the house among "exhausted negroes," or the body of Cleopatra, "stretched" on a death-bed, Gay's "delightful adventures," exhibitions of capital and sexuality, exhibitions elsewhere abstract, are here subject to a bodily demise. If the "transactions of the House" of Dombey and Son involve "most parts of the world" (843), the secure estate that replaces it depends no less on distant regions; the "hushed child" who constitutes this estate rests on the stilled body of the Orient.

Daniel Deronda and the Afterlife
of Ownership

1

*D*ANIEL DERONDA describes the most familiar idea of what it means to own in its first impression of the extraordinary estate of Sir Mallinger Grandcourt Mallinger, a property not only prodigious, but also unencumbered. The unentailed estate of the "only child" is also available to the woman he marries: Grandcourt's recessiveness charms Gwendolen Harleth with the prospect of wealth without a catch. An aura of freedom bathes in the softest light all of Gwendolen Harleth's premonitions of her coming enfranchisement, her acquisition of the title that her suitor embodies: "Adorably quiet," Grandcourt

> seemed as little a flaw in his fortunes as a lover and a husband could possibly be. Gwendolen wished to mount the chariot and drive the plunging horses herself, with a spouse by her side who would fold his arms and give her his countenance. . . . He did not appear to enjoy anything much. That was not necessary: and the less he had of particular tastes or desires, the more freedom his wife was likely to have in following hers. (173)

The freedom that Gwendolen Harleth imagines she will have when she marries an almost anonymous fortune is like the freedom that any proprietor has over his estate, according to the sense of ownership with which we are most at home.

This idea casts property as "an unconditionally complying object"[1] and possession as the power to do whatever one likes with the object possessed. During the past several centuries, liberal property theory has extended this idea of possession, enlisting it as the instrument and model for the construction of freedom in general. In an essay asserting the liberal conviction that private property defines, produces, and protects freedom, Charles A. Reich describes the foremost function of estate as the designation of a sphere of absolute discretion for its proprietor:

Property draws a circle around the activities of each private individual or organization. Within, he is master . . . property . . . create[s] zones within which the majority has to yield to the owner. Whim, caprice, irrationality and "antisocial" activities are given the protection of law.[2]

The conception of ownership that Reich expresses here, what historians of property call "absolute possession," is condensed in the vision that Gwendolen Harleth entertains of the title that she will receive from Grandcourt. The man she marries charms her with the franchise of freedom: "'You shall have whatever you like,' said Grandcourt" (349). Here, the intimacy between ownership and liberty is intensified: freedom is not only the fruit of estate; it has become its content. The title that Grandcourt offers Gwendolen consists of "what she likes"; the property that Gwendolen "gets" consists of "her choice" (351). As Alan Ryan remarks, this identification of property and freedom is

something . . . familiar in the twentieth century, namely to move from the claim that a man with property (in the usual sense) has a certain security and independence to the claim that a man with a certain security and independence has property (in an unusual sense).[3]

There is another way of describing this conception of proprietorial prerogative: the freedom *from* rule that defines the boundaries of liberal possession is the freedom *to* rule within those boundaries—"within" these boundaries, the proprietor "is master." W. B. Friedman describes the range of modern property relations as a continuum that comprehends the calibrations of mastery, "the degree of control that a physical or corporate person exercises over an aggregate of tangible things, be they land, shares, claims or powers of disposal."[4] Georg Simmel clarifies the equation of possession and power:

Just as my body is mine . . . to a higher degree than any other object because it obeys my psychic impulses more directly than any other object and because these impulses are almost completely expressed in it, so, to the same extent, every object for which this is valid is mine. The fact that one can "do what one wishes" with an object is not only a consequence of ownership but actually means that one owns it. (322)[5]

The conception of ownership I am considering here is by no means the only idea of what it means to possess, either in or outside *Daniel Deronda*. In *The Philosophy of Money*, Simmel describes rival conceptions of ownership:

In ancient northern Peru and ancient Mexico too, the tilling of the
fields—redistributed every year—was a common task. . . . Not only was
no one allowed to sell or give away his share, he lost his property if he
voluntarily travelled to other parts and did not return in time for the
cultivation of his tract of land. In the same way, the possession of a tract
of land in the ancient German marches did not yet signify that one was
a real member of the march; in order to be a full member one also
had to till the soil oneself and, as was stated in early judicial sentences,
make use of water and grazing facilities and have one's own hearth.
(304)[6]

Simmel speaks here of forms of possession defined not as the prerogative
to rule over property, but as the opposite, as submission to duties that
inhere in it. Here, obligation defines the character rather than the
boundaries of possession. This idea of ownership can be found slightly
closer to home. Lawrence Stone argues that the strict settlement of
property upon designated heirs, an arrangement enforced in England
from the seventeenth until the nineteenth century, was recognized as
the definition rather than the limitation of ownership:

It is very unlikely that even if the heir was in a position legally to break
the entail, he would in practice commonly wish to take advantage of the
opportunity to sell his inheritance. The strict settlement was an inge-
nious legal device, but it was invented by conveyancers to meet the
wishes of their clients. There was a strong sense of moral obligation felt
by most greater landowners, first that they were no more than trustees
for the transmission intact of their patrimony according to the rule of
primogeniture and second, that all their children were entitled to a
fixed and guaranteed monetary share.[7]

The conception of property as a form of duty is embodied in the story of
Deronda's discovery of his ethnicity. In a variation of the standard Victorian plot of hidden or stolen estate, revealed or returned at last to its
proper owner, Deronda's racial identity is finally disclosed to him by the
mother who had concealed it; his ancient "inheritance" is "restor[ed],"
the "robb[ery]" of his "duty" repaired (725).[8] The duty that constitutes
Deronda's racial inheritance takes shape as the nationalist project that
Mordecai sets out for him.[9] But Deronda's assumption of this duty occurs in a place and a time projected outside the novel, and it is identified
as the resurrection of an abandoned, ancient legacy: I want to suggest
that *Daniel Deronda*'s nationalist plot may be read as George Eliot's

effort to compensate for the general absence in her novel of the idea of duty-bound ownership.

By the middle of the nineteenth century, the conviction that owning involved obligations, an idea whose trace persists in the perennial odor of noblesse oblige that still wafts through the precincts of old money, is already regarded as a thing of the past. Like Simmel, Victorians discontented with the hegemony of absolute property resorted to antiquity in order to adduce examples of such estate.[10] For Eliot, interest in the forms of property that compose or signal obligation has become the exceptional passion of Enthusiasm, the charisma of the exotic, or the antiquarian's eccentric interest in "the . . . pathetic inheritance," whose "grandeur and . . . glory have become a sorrowing memory" (*DD* 415). Dorothea Casaubon's unguided efforts in *Middlemarch* to invest her fortune in good works is part of the impractical nostalgia and ethical extravagance that distinguish Eliot's heroine from her neighbors. Her hatred of her wealth and the relief she feels in relinquishing it at the end results from the fact that it is unaccompanied by any prescription for its proper use. The muteness of Dorothea Casaubon's fortune announces the disappearance of duty from the sphere of property, a disappearance that also afflicts Eliot's last hero: "Many of us complain that half our birthright is sharp duty: Deronda was more inclined to complain that he was robbed of this half" (*DD* 526).

Daniel Deronda casts this conception of ownership as a force of authority that baffles complacency or resistance; this conception visits as the "vague" "yet mastering" "something" that persuades Gwendolen Harleth to keep the necklace that she had sold and that Deronda, without her consent, retrieved for her. The link between keeping and compulsion will eventually circle around in the other direction as well: Deronda's rescue of Gwendolen's necklace originates his general "mastery" of her, thus positioning compulsion as the product as well as the cause of possession; but at first, her attachment to the man who made her keep what she wished to relinquish appears in the mere repetition of that compulsion:

> The movement of mind which led her to keep the necklace . . . came from that streak of superstition in her . . . a superstition which lingers in an intense personality even in spite of theory and science. . . . Why she should suddenly determine not to part with the necklace was not much clearer to her than why she should sometimes have been frightened to find herself in the fields alone: she had a confused state of

emotion about Deronda—was it wounded pride and resentment, or a certain awe and exceptional trust. It was something vague and yet mastering, which impelled her to this action about the necklace. There is a great deal of unmapped country within us which would have to be taken into account in an explanation of our gusts and storms. (321)

No less than the necklace itself, the affective event that prompts Gwendolen to keep it constitutes a kind of souvenir. Not for the first time, and not for the last, the induction of love takes shape as an archaic form of possession; the "superstition" that urges a woman to retain her father's necklace comes from a primitive place, part of the "unmapped country within us."

The impulse inhabiting the "unmapped country within us" resembles the inhabitants of a primordial unmapped country far from us in Wilkie Collins's *The Moonstone* (1868)—the Indians who set out to recover a sacred property, a jewel that forms the centerpiece of ancient religious obligations, from Englishmen who steal it. And insistent ownership also bears the hue of elegy: the streak of superstition retraces the mark made by "wounded wings" that Eliot mentions earlier in the novel, the "wounded wings" that "the helpless drag . . . forsakenly, and streak the shadowed moss with the red moment-hand of their own death" (228).

Such ideas of ownership are positioned in *Daniel Deronda* in the past or the future; but the idea of absolute possession, of ownership that defines it as a form of freedom or power, is the normative model that informs current conceptions of ownership in the novel. My point here is not that ownership is not restricted in *Daniel Deronda*, but that such restrictions are regarded now as something imposed on possession, rather than part of the definition of the term. Compare the notion of entailment that Stone describes, or Deronda's sense of the "duties" that he has been "robbed of," with Sir Hugo's annoyance at the entailment of his estates. Such entailment now represents an external encumbrance restricting ownership rather than the duty that defines it.

Moreover, Sir Hugo's disappointment is paradigmatic. The idea that property *should* be an "unconditionally complying object" appears in *Daniel Deronda only* in the form of its disappointment. And what is true for Eliot's novel is true generally for both literary and nonliterary efforts to represent absolute possession. Liberal economic theory invariably restricts the power of ownership, as Elizabeth Fox-Genovese and Eugene Genovese remark:

Private property never could realize itself in social policy as genuinely absolute . . . all classical liberal theorists have had to agree that property should be rendered a good deal less "absolute" than they would like— that society must place limits upon property rights.[11]

Absolute possession is never realized within the formal economy as it is represented by the theorists who promulgate it, nor is it realized in the formal economy as it is represented by *Daniel Deronda*. In order to understand why this is true for Eliot's novel, we need to consider the historical context in which the idea of absolute ownership gained hegemony: namely, the rise of capitalism.

Absolute ownership is the means and mirror of the capitalist economy; such an idea of possession enables and is enabled by an economy characterized by the hegemony of commodity exchange. Thus Marx draws together a long line of thought about the relation between private property and market economics when, in a famous scene from *Capital*, he sets up the rights of ownership as a kind of puppet show, strung along by the circulation requirements of the commodity form. Since

commodities cannot themselves go to market and perform exchanges in their own right, . . . they must, therefore, have recourse to their guardians, who are the possessors of commodities. . . . In order that these objects may enter into relation with each other as commodities, their guardians must place themselves in relation to one another as persons whose will resides in those objects, and must behave in such a way that each does not appropriate the commodity of the other, and alienate his own, except through an act to which both parties consent. The guardians must therefore recognize each other as owners of private property. (179)[12]

Daniel Deronda neatly sketches the relation between the malleability and marketability of property in the passage where the princess gives her son away: "Take my boy and bring him up an Englishman," the princess instructs Sir Hugo Mallinger, who responds in kind, "declar[ing] that he would pay money to have such a boy" (697). The mother's remarkable assertion of the right to alienate her child is followed by the boy's appearance as monetary value. When property can be *sold* in the root sense of the term—given—then it can be sold in its more recent and recognizable sense as well.

If the idea of absolute property furnishes the means of the marketplace, the force of the marketplace, in turn, defines the boundary of absolute possession. With the hegemony of the commodity form, the hazy vision of proprietorial prerogative resolves into the shape salient for an exchange economy, the prerogative that P. S. Attiyah mentions: "The most important freedom of property for a market economy is the freedom to sell. A market economy demands that property be freely transferable so that it can pass from hand to hand."[13]

By the middle of the nineteenth century, the right to alienate has become the centerpiece of proprietorial prerogative; as John Stuart Mill indicates, "the power to bestow" has become the sine qua non of the right of ownership:

> The ownership of a thing cannot be looked upon as complete without the power of bestowing it, at death or during life, at the owner's pleasure: and all the reasons, which recommend that private property should exist, recommend *pro tanto* this extension of it.[14]

The conviction that the right to alienate is an inherent and characterizing constituent of proprietorial prerogative manifests itself in the escalating inability of nineteenth-century Anglo-American culture to imagine forms of possessive power that stop short of the "power to bestow." In her famous summary of laws pertaining to married women, Barbara Bodichon designates the husband's legal claim to his wife as just such a form of ownership:

> A married woman's body belongs to her husband; she is in his custody, and he can enforce his right by a writ of habeas corpus. But . . . the belief that a man can rid himself of his wife by going through the farce of a sale, and exhibiting his wife with a halter round her neck is a vulgar error. This disgusting exhibition, which has often been seen in our country, is a misdemeanor, and can be punished with fine and imprisonment. The author of a recent publication asserts that a man may lend his wife; a man may not lend, let out, or sell his wife; such transactions are considered as being against public decency, and are misdemeanors.[15]

But if the husband's possession of his wife does not include the right to "lend, let out, or sell" her, Bodichon's account here exhibits the widely held belief that it does. And this "disgusting exhibition" is an instance of a more general inability or refusal to recognize forms of ownership that do not include the right to sell. The widely manifested belief that proprietorial right per se, including, most acutely, the proprietorial right in persons, necessarily involves "the power to bestow" surpasses the bounds of "vulgar error"; it also appears in the inability of antebellum

American jurisprudence to sustain a theoretical separation between the possession of slaves and the possession of commodities, as well as the inability of postbellum American jurisprudence to produce a coherent justification for its general refusal to endorse the assertion that people have an unrestricted right to sell their interest in themselves.[16]

In *Daniel Deronda*—and not only there—the centrality, for possession, of the "power to bestow" often asserts itself in the utter identification of proprietorial prerogative with this power; an owner's power over his or her property becomes, simply, an owner's power to alienate it: "If Sir Hugo Mallinger could have done as he liked with his estates, he would have left them to . . . Mr Deronda" (378). The testimony of our own consciousness may furnish the last word here: what does our now stripped sense of owning usually mean, other than the right to sell?

.   .   .   .   .

An idea of proprietorial power reposited primarily, even exclusively, in the "power to bestow" may dwell in the happiest alliance with the market economy, but it does so by severely restricting the boundless ambitions for mastery that form a deep part of the ideological heritage of possession. We can begin to assess the infinitude of these ambitions by glancing at the Physiocrats, whose emphatic expressions of how much it means to own are regarded by some historians as the first thorough articulation of absolute property. "The property the physiocrats had in mind," Elizabeth Fox-Genovese and Eugene Genovese remark, "predated society." "Property was sacrosanct, natural, divine. . . . It constituted a presocial right." For the Physiocrats, ownership helps define the charmed circle of humanity's "immutable essence": "Material possession, unequal though it may be [is, according to the Physiocrats] inseparable from the essence of humanity."[17]

The power of ownership has no history. It is not just that the right to possess inhabits the magic place outside of history that Marxists call the sphere of ideology; absolute possession itself transcends the limits of temporality: the power of owning, according to the sense we are considering here, is supposed to last forever. In the Victorian novel, this great expectation makes its most memorable appearance in the severe shock or irritation that always comes when property fails to endure. This includes the various quotidian disappointments that afflict the property owner in Eliot's fiction who crosses the bar of marketplace possession, the inexorable temporal limit that constricts proprietorial prerogative when that prerogative is defined as the opportunity to alienate. The sense of "imperfect mastery" that "clings and gnaws within Grandcourt" (399) when he is compelled to petition his mistress to return the diamonds that he gave her refers by negation to the expectation of endless prerogative, an expectation inevitably disappointed by the temporal form cast upon possession when it is readied for the marketplace. Such possession will always upset the expectation of enduring proprietorial power, because it can be exercised only once: expenditure is an event rather than a condition; the alienation of property is an irreversible act, at once the realization and termination of ownership's potence.

Such "imperfect mastery" is signaled in *Middlemarch* by the dead hand of Peter Featherstone, who, despite cunning efforts to maintain control of what he owns, is finally compelled to relax his grip: "Peter Featherstone was dead, with his right hand clasping the keys, and his left hand lying on the heap of notes and gold."[18] But the lethal loosening of Featherstone's grasp began with the falling of his shocked hand the night before, when his servant refused to enable him to change his will:

"Not do it? I tell you, you must," said the old man, his voice beginning to shake under the shock of this resistance. . . .
     He let his hand fall, and . . . beg[an] to cry childishly. (261)

Having given herself to Grandcourt, Gwendolen "could not go backward now" (*DD* 355); she is "irrevocably engaged" (356). "Her capability of rectitude told her again and again that she had no right to complain of her contract, or to withdraw from it" (665).[19] Solemnity greets her announcement that she has engaged herself to Grandcourt ("'My darling child!', said Mrs. Davilow, with a surprise that was rather solemn than glad"), a solemnity that reflects the first economic rule that a "spoiled child" must learn: what is given can't be taken back. Once performed, the power of owning falls into the irretrievable past. As if to dramatize this, the act of owning, once performed, is not merely cast into the sphere of anteriority, it works to construct it. Grandcourt, by giving his mistress his mother's diamonds, "had made a past for himself which was stronger than any he could impose. He must ask for the diamonds which he had promised to Gwendolen" (294).

Marketplace possession, accordingly, is throned in a reign of potentiality, prior to the actual exercise of the power that defines and ends it. This is the region where Featherstone seeks to linger; Grandcourt inhabits it while pondering his uncle's offer to buy one of his estates. Gwendolen enjoys the same ephemeral dominium more fleetingly when, presented with Grandcourt's offer of marriage, the marriage that the novel unflinchingly calls a "contract" where she "sells herself" (733), her waning sense of power is briefly reanimated by a taste of the pleasures of absolute ownership.

She invites Grandcourt's efforts to "to bribe [her] will," because

> Firmness hath its appetite and craves
> The stronger lure, more strongly to resist
> Would know the touch of gold to fling it off
> Scent wine to feel its lip the soberer;
> Behold soft byssus, ivory, and plumes
> To say "They're fair, but I will none of them,"
> And flout Enticement in the very face.　　　　(332)

The evil hour of temptation forms a virtual allegory for the ephemeral Eden of proprietorial prerogative:

> "You will tell me now, I hope, that Mrs Davilow's loss of fortune will not trouble you further. You will trust me to prevent it from weighing upon her. You will give me the claim to provide against that."
>
> The little pauses and refined drawlings with which this speech was uttered, gave time for Gwendolen to go through the dream of a life. As the words penetrated her, they had the effect of a draught of wine, which suddenly makes all things easier, desirable things not so wrong, and people in general less disagreeable. She had a momentary phantasmal love for this man who chose his words so well, and who was a mere incarnation of delicate homage. Repugnance, dread, scruples—these were dim as remembered pains, while she was already tasting relief under the immediate pain of hopelessness. She imagined herself already springing to her mother, and being playful again. Yet when Grandcourt had ceased to speak, there was an instant in which she was conscious of being at the turning of the ways. (347)

The ambitions of mastery that inhere in the idea of absolute ownership can be sensed here in Gwendolen's feeling of the compliance of others; and if the images housed by this dream refract the power of possession, its anticipatory structure mimics the situation of absolute ownership. Just as the glow of power that warms possession is cast upon it by the potential exercise of mastery before which it is poised, Gwendolen's fantasy stages future possibilities as immediate pleasures of power.

The ominous sound of the knowledge that descends when Grandcourt is done with his proposal knells the limit of absolute possession: "When Grandcourt had ceased to speak, there was an instant in which she was conscious of being at the turning of the ways." Since its realization is its end, absolute ownership can be sustained only by deferring its ultimate exercise. Only by "eluding a direct appeal" can "Gwendolen recover . . . some of her self-possession" (346).

Eliot's novel registers and intensifies the capitalist construction of absolute ownership by casting the exercise of the prerogative that defines such ownership as the terminus of a trajectory, the inevitable end of an inexorable progression. In *Daniel Deronda*, economic mastery is everywhere coaxed to what we can call, in both senses of the term, its end. According to Eliot's account, possession lives in the space between a question and its answer, between the calling of a name and its recognition: "'You accept my devotion?' said Grandcourt. . . . 'Yes,' came as gravely from Gwendolen's lips as if she had been answering to her name in a court of justice." By "sell[ing] herself," Gwendolen Harleth merely acknowledges and completes an inexorable sentence.

As we have seen, *Daniel Deronda* dramatizes the trajectory of proprietorial prerogative by merging this movement with Eve's tragic steps. Gwendolen's self-possession rehearses the fate that it carefully echoes when it seeks to confront temptation and "flout Enticement in the very face." She sells herself to Grandcourt in a late emanation of Eve's trade, "not that she could still imagine herself plucking the fruits of life without suspicion of their core" (333).

And if it likens the exercise of proprietorial prerogative to the unfolding of a mythic doom, *Daniel Deronda* also affiliates the trajectory of proprietorial prerogative with the nonsectarian teleological undertow of narrative itself.[20] One of Eliot's most considered images nears the surface when she describes the form of Gwendolen Harleth's entrapment, the cage that draws her to the end of her self-possession, to the "contract" with Grandcourt, as a "net." This figure recalls the "web" that is Eliot's figure for the resolution of novelistic narrative. Here is Eliot's famous defense of her method in *Middlemarch*: "I at least have so much to do in unravelling certain human lots, and seeing how they were woven and unwoven, that all the light I can command must be concentrated on this particular web" (116). The resemblance between the plot of the novel and the net that draws Gwendolen forward to the end of her self-possession signals their deep collaboration. In *Daniel Deronda* the inexorable sentence that urges the proprietor to the terminus of possession joins the force that a reader feels in the urge to get to the end.

The intimacy between the telos of ownership and the telos of narrative surpasses their end rhyme when Deronda's mother calls fulfilling the dictates of proprietorial will a matter of finishing a story: "If I tell everything—if I deliver up everything—what else can be demanded of me?" (702). And this identification extends beyond the particular predicament of Deronda's mother. Narrative drive is merged most comprehensively with the trajectory of absolute ownership through the habits of Lapidoth, a character whom the novel makes into a screen upon which it projects its own teleological dynamic:

> By no distinct change of resolution, rather by a dominance of desire, like the thirst of the drunkard—it so happened that in passing the table his fingers fell noiselessly on the ring, and he found himself in the passage with the ring in his hand. It followed that he put on his hat and quitted the house. The possibility of again throwing himself on his children receded into the indefinite distance, and before he was out of the square his sense of haste had concentrated itself on selling the ring and getting on shipboard. (678)

Lapidoth's little narrative of ownership takes on the larger status of narrative generally: this is not only a story, it is also the figure of story itself. What some observers of the form call the bare elements of narrative work through the character of Lapidoth here,[21] a sequence of events that we recognize as the rhetorical elements of a story ("it so happened," "it followed"), that serve as prelude to a motivating conclusion. The elements of narrative emerge into view in this passage as determining entities, overwhelming the specific agency and affect of the character enmeshed in it.

This instance of what Neil Hertz describes as the "oddly generic" quality of the weird prose that surrounds Lapidoth is consonant with the labor of embodiment he is made to perform generally in *Daniel Deronda*:[22] to serve as the site upon which the impersonal, even invisible force of narrative and specifically the novel's own narrative can be apprehended. The disappearance of Lapidoth's consciousness is the disappearance of a text, the "widening margin where consciousness once was"; his habitual dissimulation, "reflecting every phase of . . . feeling with mimetic susceptibility" (810), likens him to the realist novel; most important for us, the "numbers and movements that seemed to make the very tissue of Lapidoth's consciousness" (849) identify him with the numbers and movements that mark the progress of that text.

And if the dominance of desire that works through Lapidoth is the teleological demand of novelistic narrative, it is at the same time the inevitable performance of proprietorial prerogative, the "sense of haste" that "concentrate[s] itself . . . on selling the ring." And this is not the only place in the novel where the fascination of owning takes on the form and force of the demand to complete a story. Who are the entranced gamblers crowding the first chapter of *Daniel Deronda*, if not the "attention bent" (36) readers of the sensational serial novel, unable to stop before they have reached its generic ending?

> While every single player differed markedly from every other, there was a certain uniform expression which had the effect of a mask—as if they had all eaten of some root that for the time compelled the brains of each to the same narrow monotony of action. (37)

The "moment hand" drama of fascinated ownership ("each time her stake was swept off she doubled it. . . . Such a drama takes no long while to play out; development and catastrophe can often be measured by nothing clumsier than the moment hand") is a spectacular enactment of the fate that always shadows possession. When the novel makes the "development and catastrophe" of ownership the "development and catastrophe" of narrative, it dramatizes their common character: possession, like narrative, is prologue to its own demise.

2

Eliot's last novel isn't principally about a struggle for estates or diamonds or "shares" or cash; nor even, as we will see in a moment, is it primarily concerned with the ownership of women: here the exigencies of ownership, elsewhere in Victorian literature the star of the show, have been pushed to the sidelines. What property there is in *Daniel Deronda* nobody cares about very much, certainly not the novel's hero, "sustained by three or five percent on capital which somebody else has battled for" (225); and certainly not the novel's villain, who quite accurately notes that he "doesn't care a curse about . . . money." Even the novel's victim, after a brief bout of pleasure in the "almost incredible fulfillment about to be given to her girlish dreams" of "walking through her own furlong of corridors and under her own ceilings of an out-of-sight loftiness, where her own painted Spring was shedding painted flowers and her own foreshortened Zephyrs were blowing their trumpets over her" (404), loses all interest in her title. Grandcourt's shrewd sadism errs only once, when he imagines that he can torment his wife with the knowledge that most of his property will go to someone else when he dies. Afflicted by the sense of "imperfect mastery," possession isn't very interesting in *Daniel Deronda*, because it can't be interesting for long.

The yearning for more tenacious mastery must look elsewhere. Grandcourt is roused from his "flaccid" (145) indifference, "the grandly passive kind which consists in the inheritance of land" (644), by the prospect of "mastering" Gwendolen: "His strongest wish was to be completely master of this creature" (346); this yearning "st[ings] him into a keenness of interest such as he had not known for years." Durable dominion does not inhere in the possession of objects, even when these objects are people; it works instead through psychological domination.

Everyone remembers Grandcourt's "empire of fear," the intangible "mastery" that baffles his bride's sunlit regency of surfaces:

> Her husband had gained a mastery which she could no more resist than she could have resisted the benumbing effect from the touch of a torpedo. Gwendolen's will had seemed imperious in its small girlish sway; but it was the will of a creature with a large discourse of imaginative fears: a shadow would have been enough to relax its hold. And she had found a will like that of a crab or a boa-constrictor which goes on pinching or crushing without alarm at thunder. Not that Grandcourt was without calculation of the intangible effects which were the chief means of his mastery; indeed he had a surprising acuteness in detecting the situation of feeling in Gwendolen which made her proud and rebellious spirit dumb and helpless before him. (477–78)

Grandcourt can exert mastery over his property only once, but the mastery he exerts over "a creature with a large discourse of imaginative fears" is continuous; while the power of the proprietorial will is subject to punctuation, the power of the will that takes as its field of operations the "situation of feeling" "*goes on* pinching or crushing" (my emphasis).

The operation of this ongoing power in *Daniel Deronda* is not confined to its villain. For his share, the novel's hero exerts a "vague yet mastering" (321) effect on Gwendolen's "situation of feeling."

> Her anger had changed into a superstitious dread—due, perhaps, to the coercion he had exercised over her thought—lest that first interference of his in her life might foreshadow some future influence. It is of such stuff that superstitions are commonly made: an intense feeling about ourselves which makes the evening star shine at us with a threat, and the blessing of a beggar encourage us. (374–75)

The force that Deronda exerts upon Gwendolen's inner life is prophetic in every sense; the memory of the original "coercion he had exercised over her thought" gives way to the vague prospect of further intervention, the "dread" of an undisclosed act of influence. In the turn of metaphor that takes place in the second sentence of this passage, the possibility of realizing and thus exhausting the force of futurity grows more remote; the picture of things to come grows dimmer, more distant, and thus more enduring: the comparative specificity of Gwendolen's apprehension that Deronda might intervene in her life again dissolves before the bare prophecy of "threat" or "encourage[ment]." Within Gwendolen's "situation of feeling," Deronda's authority, like Grandcourt's "empire of fear," takes on a form of mastery with no end in sight. It is, of course, no accident that the "situation of feeling" upon which such mastery works is specifically feminine. I will return in the next section to describe this specificity.

Late in the novel, a sick prophet exults in his "trust" in the hero:

> "You must be not only a hand to me, but a soul—believing my belief—being moved by my reasons—hoping my hope—seeing the vision I point to—beholding a glory where I behold it!"—Mordecai had taken a step nearer as he spoke, and now laid his hand on Deronda's arm with a tight grasp; his face little more than a foot off had something like a pale flame in it—an intensity of reliance that acted as a peremptory claim. (557)

The shift in grip that takes place between *Middlemarch* and *Daniel Deronda*, the shift from the futile hand of the dead proprietor to the enduring grasp of the dying prophet, and the "white hand" of the emperor of fear, measures a movement from economic to psychic mastery, a movement that occurs constantly within *Daniel Deronda* itself. It appears, for example, very early in the novel, when Eliot's glance drifts from a detail of the estate Grandcourt owns to the internal agonies that he incites:

> Mr Henleigh Mallinger Grandcourt was at his breakfast-table with Mr Lush. Everything around them was agreeable: the summer air through the open windows, at which the dogs could walk in from the old green turf on the lawn; the soft, purplish colouring of the park beyond, stretching towards a mass of bordering wood; the still life in the room which seemed the stiller for its sober antiquated elegance, as if it kept a conscious, well-bred silence, unlike the restlessness of vulgar furniture. . . . The dogs—half-a-dozen of various kinds were moving lazily

in and out . . . all except Fetch, the beautiful liver-coloured water-span-iel, which sat with its fore-paws firmly planted and its expressive brown face turned upward, watching Grandcourt with unshaken con-stancy. . . . He held in his lap a tiny Maltese dog with a tiny silver collar and bell, and when he had a hand unused by cigar or coffee-cup, it rested on this small parcel of animal warmth. I fear that Fetch was jeal-ous, and wounded that her master gave her no word or look; at last it seemed that she could bear this neglect no longer, and she gently put her large silky paw on her master's leg. Grandcourt looked at her with unchanged face for half a minute, and then took the trouble to lay down his cigar while he lifted the unimpassioned Fluff close to his chin and gave it caressing pats, all the while gravely watching Fetch, who, poor thing, whimpered interruptedly, as if trying to repress that sign of discontent. (160–61)

Fetch's "expressive brown face" looks forward, of course, to the tor-ment that both his mistress and his wife suffer at Grandcourt's "white hand[s]." More generally, the shift of this passage from the situation of the furniture Grandcourt owns to the "situation of feeling" that he se-cures predicts the course of power's career in Eliot's last novel.

We can catch the move from the prerogative of title to the force that works along the pulses of the psyche in the animation of the will that takes place everywhere in *Daniel Deronda*. It occurs almost accidentally when Eliot describes the "dependancy" of Grandcourt's mistress:

[Lydia Glasher] was absolutely dependant on Grandcourt; for though he had been always liberal in expenses for her . . . [h]e had said that he would never settle anything except by will . . . the mere facts of their relation to each other, the melancholy position of this woman who de-pended on his will, made a standing banquet for his delight in dominat-ing. (387–89)

The displacement of economic by psychic mastery appears when the rep-etition of "will" does more than merely repeat its first meaning. If the second "will" upon which Lydia Glasher depends here refers to the legal instrument by which a proprietor determines the disposition of his es-tates, it also looks forward to the intangible grasp of the mind, the "will like that of a crab or a boa-constrictor which goes on pinching or crush-ing." This migration is all the more impressively insistent for being made almost imperceptible by Eliot's novel. The displacement of the limited prerogative of ownership by ongoing psychological mastery, the displacement suggested by the move from will to will, takes on the force of mechanical necessity, like the alteration of a word's meaning that results inevitably when we say it again.

Gwendolen Harleth "sells" her "truthfulness and sense of justice" to Grandcourt, "so that he held them throttled into silence" (733), but his ongoing rule over these things gets started only when that sale is suspended. Grandcourt alludes to this sale only once in the novel, in a passage where Gwendolen is irritated by the thought of her deceit and injustice.

> "Are you as kind to me as I am to you?" said Grandcourt, looking into her eyes with his narrow gaze.
>
> She was conscious of having received so much, that her sense of command was checked, and sank away . . . it was as if she had consented to mount a chariot where another held the reins; and it was not in her nature to leap out in the eyes of the world. . . . With a sort of mental shiver, she resolutely changed her mental attitude. There had been a little pause, during which she had not turned away her eyes; and with a sudden break into a smile, she said—
>
> "If I were as kind to you as you are to me, that would spoil your generosity: it would no longer be as great as it could be—and it is that now." (373)

Refusing to return goods in kind for all that she has received, Gwendolen arrests the execution of an exchange of property which Grandcourt almost mentions here. All that Gwendolen receives fails to secure for its donor the "kindn[ess]" to which he would be entitled in return if the rule of exchange were in place. But obligation is not evaded by the suspension of exchange; rather, it is rendered infinite.[23] Grandcourt may lose, for a moment, his entitlement, but he gains an interminable kingdom instead—a form of power that takes place in an imagination shadowed by his generosity. Gwendolen imagines embarking on an excursion where Grandcourt holds the reins, an excursion with no end in sight.

3

Daniel Deronda distinguishes the ongoing power that exerts itself upon the "conscious[ness]" of the subjected from the power available to the marketplace version of absolute possession. Paradoxically, such psychological mastery also retraces the fundamental lineaments of absolute ownership. In *Slavery and Social Death*, Orlando Patterson excavates the subterranean figure of slavery buried beneath the original conception of absolute property, devised by Roman law: "It is not the condition of slavery that must be defined in terms of absolute notions of property, as is often attempted; rather it is the notion of absolute property that must be explained in terms of ancient Roman slavery." According to Patterson's account, the category of "dominium or absolute ownership," a "fiction that was to haunt continental Western law for the next two thousand years," was constructed "to define one of the most rapidly expanding sources of wealth, namely slaves."

Patterson suggests that the notion of absolute property arose in the late Roman Empire as a means of distinguishing the slave from the citizen:

> Given the number of slaves in the Roman midst, it was vitally important that the issue of their status be settled. An unambiguous way had to be found for differentiating human beings classified as chattel from human beings classified as nonchattel. It should be obvious to all that any confusion on the matter would have been socially disastrous.[24]

Unlike Greece, Rome had no recourse to insuperable ethnic or class barriers that would enable it to sustain the distinction between slaves and citizens, and thus

> had no choice but to turn to law for social clarification. However, when the Romans of the expanding slave economy of the late republic turned to the ancient proprietary action (the *legis actio sacramento in rem*), they saw all too clearly that this essentially relativistic principle of property would not do as a means of distinguishing slaves from other persons. In other words, they saw clearly what any modern Anglo-American lawyer or Ashanti elder would have seen, that all human beings can be the object of property.

To distinguish between the slave and other forms of human property, "the Romans invented the legal fiction of dominium or absolute ownership."

> More than just a relation between a person and a thing, dominium was absolute power. And this absolute power involved not simply the capacity to derive the full economic value of a thing, to use (usus) and enjoy its fruits (fructus), as well as "to use it up" (ab-usus), to alienate it, but perhaps most significantly, as the Danish legal historian C. W. Westrup

notes, it has the psychological meaning "of inner power over a thing beyond mere control." If it is difficult to explain why the Romans would want to invent the idea of a relation between a person and a thing (an almost metaphysical notion, quite at variance with the Roman way of thinking in other areas), it becomes impossible to comprehend why they should want inner psychic power over it unless we understand that, for most purposes, the "thing" on their minds was a slave. (31)

And the genealogy that Patterson traces here suggests itself in various constructions of absolute possession. It is suggested, for example, in the term most consistently invoked by Anglo-American legal and literary discourses to designate such ownership: "mastery." Even a rapid review of the legal language that defines absolute possession signals the dependence of this category on domination. Blackstone's canonical account, for example, relies upon the implicit metaphor of the relation between lord and serf as a model for the relation between owner and owned. Possession, according to Blackstone's emphatic formulation, is "that sole and despotic dominion which one man claims and exercises over the external things of the world."[25]

The subjective shape that Patterson discerns at the core of the inaugural form of absolute possession, the subjective shape that subsequent constructions of the form have unfailingly adumbrated, dramatizes an argument I have been seeking to make all along, an argument for the apprehension of a deeper intimacy between the sphere of the formal economy and the shapes of the psychic. These zones have generally been kept rigorously separate, even by efforts to articulate relations and resemblances between them. I have in mind here the work that has arisen from the thought of Marx and Weber, and their psychoanalytically inflected variants, which league the workings of the formal economy and the workings of subjectivity in terms of mimesis and cooperation, or, conversely, which assert the disarticulation of the formal economy and the workings of subjectivity, casting them in relations of difference and interference. At least in the case of one core constituent of the capitalist economy, we can recognize a more radical entanglement. Psychic domination does not merely reflect or support private ownership; it was there from the start. If mastery must migrate from the bounds of estate, it is only to make durable the spirit of subjection that defines it in the first place.

But if the displacement of ownership by psychological domination in *Daniel Deronda* recovers the archaic form of proprietorial prerogative,

95

this displacement also describes a version of the thoroughly modern formation of power that Michel Foucault has made familiar to us.[26] I have traced a novel's account of something like the sublimation of power that Foucault describes in his later work, according to which the visible violence, ceremonies, and contracts dictated by law are dispersed during the modern period into more tactful and ongoing procedures, outside the official shapes of coercion. While the armies of the law are always terminable, residing finally in the power to kill—"death is [such] power's limit, the moment that escapes it"[27]—nothing stops the "ghostly army" that emerges from them. And if, as we have seen, the sublimation of power that the novel describes takes place in the shift from the constrained claims of possession to ongoing forms of power entertained by the psyche, I want to argue now that this is another way of saying that they participate in an ongoingness achieved by the novel itself.

For *Daniel Deronda*, ongoing mastery is an ongoing story. The infinite power that rises out of ownership, the mastery that takes Gwendolen Harleth's "situation of feeling" as the site of its interminable operations, consists specifically of "fantasies [that] move within her like ghosts" (668), fantasies of subjection that resonate through her mind, fantasies that end always before the prospect of further exertions of the mastery that is their source. The "mere will" (187) finds its satisfaction only in refusing to achieve the aim toward which it is projected: "[A] languor of intention . . . came over Grandcourt, like a fit of diseased numbness, when an end seemed within easy reach: to desist then when all expectation was to the contrary, became [a] gratification of mere will" (187). This "mere will," whose confinement is figured by the proprietor's failed grasp, finds its mansion in pensive narratives lodged in the mind of the dominated, echoes and effects of the infinitely "slow sentence" of mastery. While the end of proprietorial prerogative can be delayed only briefly, this sentence of mastery can be suspended indefinitely.[28]

Grandcourt's ghostly hand, taking up the scepter of power that falls from the grasp of ownership, houses itself in his wife's fancy as the sign of an endless regime: "That white hand of his . . . was capable, she fancied, of clinging round her neck and threatening to throttle her" (481). Gwendolen Grandcourt's fancy entertains the mute promise of violence reposited throughout the novel in "that white hand" by announcing that threat rather than by realizing and thus exhausting it.

Sometimes the endless story of mastery consists of the "imaginary annihilation of the detested object":

The intensest form of hatred is that rooted in fear, which compels to silence, and drives vehemence into a constructive vindictiveness, an imaginary annihilation of the detested object, something like the hidden rites of vengeance with which the persecuted have made a dark vent for their rage, and soothed their suffering into dumbness. Such hidden rites went on in the secrecy of Gwendolen's mind, but not with soothing effect—rather with the effect of a struggling terror. (737)

Unlike the "hidden rites of vengeance" through which "the persecuted" manage to extinguish the spoken effects of their persecutors, Gwendolen's imagined extinction of mastery ends where it begins, in a "struggling terror," poised again at a moment preceding the realization of an awful potence that terror, by definition, anticipates.

Her efforts to fantasize the termination of such power always conclude, or fail to conclude, in this way: "a fiercely impulsive deed, committed as in a dream" ends with

the palsy of a new terror—a white dead face from which she was ever trying to flee and for ever held back. . . . The thought of his dying would not subsist: it turned as with a dream-change into the terror that she should die with his throttling fingers on her neck avenging that thought. (737–38, 668–69)

These dreams fail in their intention, ceasing only with the prophecy of further exertions of the mastery they aim to abolish. Such stories of mastery thus evade the temporal limit of the power they displace, the regime of absolute possession, fastened to a trajectory that achieves inevitably the terminus that defines it. Ranged at the distance of an inch as good as a mile from the borders of proprietorial prerogative, the stories of the subjugated express but never exhaust the mastery that works through them. Such stories are an instance of the "quite new mechanisms," that Foucault describes, "quite new mechanisms," "irreducible to the representations of law"; such stories complete, by failing always to complete, the ambitions of mastery reposited in the "representations of law . . . a power that was centered around deduction . . . and death."[29]

D. A. Miller locates closing scenes in *Middlemarch* like the ones that end, or fail to end, Mrs. Grandcourt's fantasies, "scenes [that] commit [their] closural status to the very processes that define the narratable." These scenes, stationed everywhere at the ending boundaries of *Middlemarch* and of the nineteenth-century English novel generally, reflect, according to Miller, "the suspensive and dispersive logic of narrative" that works always to defer the end that is also always their aim: "It is as if the novelist could not help seeing the persistence of the narratable even in its closure."[30] The persistence of the narratable renders novels pensive and power endless.

In my investigation of *Little Dorrit* and *Dombey and Son*, I argued that women were enlisted as a form of estate that replaced insecure marketplace property. Correlatively, the afterlife of ownership that appears in *Daniel Deronda* depends upon a feminine psyche. The dread that characterizes and constitutes the pensive narratives I have examined, the fantasies that achieve the ambition of absolute ownership, is the dread of a woman: Gillian Beer notes that Eliot, participating in a general cultural construction, "premises the power of fear—the capacity for dread—as a particular condition of women's experience and potentiality. . . . Fear is of all emotions that which most takes its life from the future." As Beer notes, a wide variety of Victorian discourses cast dread as a primarily feminine feature:

> Incommensurate or irrational fear—hysteria—has been traditionally associated with women and particularly with pregnancy. . . . The connection had by no means been abandoned by Victorian medical theory. For example, W. B. Carpenter in *Principles of Mental Physiology with their Applications to the Training and Discipline of the Mind and the Study of Morbid Conditions* (1874) has no entry for women or female in the index or for their particular conditions. But when he discusses hysteria and "general exaltation of sensibility" he shifts from the masculine gender he uses elsewhere to describe the patient, and instead refers to "she" and "her."[31]

Thus a Victorian construction of femininity is enlisted in *Daniel Deronda* as the site for the exercise of proprietorial prerogative, a site that evades the limits imposed by the marketplace.

The power that displaces and perfects proprietorial prerogative lingers at the moment prior to its realization, in a dread like the thought of a lethal virus that has yet to reach its conclusion:

> Every slow sentence of [Grandcourt's] speech had a terrific mastery in it for Gwendolen's nature. If the low tones had come from a physician telling her that her symptoms were those of a fatal disease, and prognosticating its course, she could not have been more helpless against the argument that lay in it. (655)

This is the language of a regime that manages to baffle the anticipatory logic that draws its predecessor to its close; exceeding at once the boundaries of property and the novel, this is the afterlife of ownership, the ghost and prophet of the now-endless exertions of mastery.

The Miser's Two Bodies: Sexual Perversity and the Flight from Capital in *Silas Marner*

1

IN *Silas Marner* the exodus of property from marketplace to household is as easy as *ABC*; the avenue of this exodus, elsewhere a circuitous route available only through elaborate pains of detection, here seems the straightest of paths. *Silas Marner* is the abridged edition of a story whose complicated details we have seen sprawled across the Victorian novel: when a girl's golden hair replaces a miser's lost gold, the complex lines of flight through which estate migrates from the formal economy to the household are simplified to the scheme of a fairy tale.

And even the generations of schoolchildren assigned to read *Silas Marner* could trace in it an elementary version of the insurance scheme that I have assessed before: the daughter who replaces the miser's money is property that transcends the risky business of commodity ownership. The miser's money is always alienable, but the father's "claim" to the "little 'un'"[1] endures any threat of loss; the system of exchange that propels the plot of the story passes over the door of this estate: while the daughter that one brother abandons to the miser compensates for the gold that another brother stole from him, she remains his even when the money is restored and the natural father seeks to reclaim her, for just as "there's debts we can't pay like money debts" (236), there are claims we can't lose like property, which can always be brought to market.

For all its simplicity, though, this story has a twist: the firm footing that the weaver eventually finds in a father's claim comes on the heels of another, more slippery escape from the sphere of exchange. Unlike others we have encountered, Silas Marner's first attempt to save property from the vicissitudes of the cash nexus is less a transfer of investments away from commodities than a translation of them, less the replacement of the commodity form than an effort to renovate it: "He would on no account have exchanged those coins, which had become his familiars, for other coins with unknown faces" (68).

The insecurity of the miser's hold on these beloved figures is only one of its dangers. His valorization of the coins constitutes a threat not only to the safe property associated with the home, but also to the propriety that is expected to dwell there. If the specter of illicit sexuality attaches itself to the circulation of commodities in novels like *Little Dorrit* and *Dombey and Son*, it attaches itself to the effort to suspend it in *Silas Marner*.

A specter we can begin to trace in a campaign on behalf of family values whose directness is unlike any other in an Eliot novel: forsaking her customary tact, Eliot fills the story with simple maxims and paeans promoting a life with wives and children and emphatic caveats about a life without them. A faith in the family she is elsewhere content confiding to the implications of her narrative is here urged, and urged again, as conspicuous doctrine. Pulling out the stops, Eliot pours her formidable but usually discreet didactic energy into a straightforward channel of simple exhortation: "The Squire's wife had died long ago, and the Red House was without that presence of the wife and mother which is the fountain of wholesome love and fear in parlour and kitchen" (72); men without women inhabit houses "destitute of any hallowing charm" (73) and filled instead with the "scent of flat ale" (73); men without women live in a region barren of the "sweet flower of courtesy" (121); men without women dwell in a twilight zone of tedium vitae whose only source of light is the memory of what is lost to them:

> Pass[ing] their days in the half-listless gratification of senses dulled by monotony . . . perhaps the love of some sweet maiden, the image of purity, order, and calm, had opened their eyes to the vision of a life in which the days would not seem too long, even without rioting; but the maiden was lost, and the vision passed away, and then what was left to them, especially when they had become too heavy for the hunt . . . ? (79)

The pains that patient Dolly Winthrop takes to teach the errant weaver the work of raising a child are surely no greater than the pains that *Silas Marner* takes to promote it. A heart of stone, or at least one made weary by the current residuals of advertising strategies already unfolded in *Silas Marner*, would be necessary to resist the sight of

> Eppie, discoursing cheerfully to her own small boot, which she was using as a bucket to convey the water into a deep hoof-mark, while her little naked foot was planted comfortably on a cushion of olive-green mud. A red-headed calf was observing her with alarmed doubt through the opposite hedge. (187)

It is hard to imagine how the difference between the wholesome delights of the semitraditional family life Silas Marner manages to sustain with his stepdaughter and the debilitating bleakness of his money love could be remarked more blatantly or more often. The fine calibrations of a moral scale able to weigh with utmost precision the specific densities of characters as various as Mr. Farebrother, Nicholas Bulstrode, and the Princess Halm-Eberstein are abandoned for the blunt dichotomy of the primer when Eliot comes to assess the evil of the gold and the goodness of the child:

> The gold had kept his thoughts in an ever-repeated circle, leading to nothing beyond itself; but Eppie was an object compacted of changes and hopes that forced his thoughts onward . . . to the new things that would come with the coming years, when [she] would have learned to understand how her father Silas cared for her. . . . The gold had asked that he should sit weaving longer and longer, deafened and blinded more and more to all things except the monotony of his loom and the repetition of his web; but Eppie called him away from his weaving, and made him think all its pauses a holiday, re-awakening his senses with her fresh life. (184)

Silas Marner's commerce with his gold looks less dull in an earlier description, where its deviation from the purity and order of traditional familial arrangements verges on forms of sexuality that both Victorian and contemporary champions of those arrangements apprehend as enemy number one:

> It was pleasant to him to feel them in his palm, and look at their bright faces. . . . He handled them . . . till their form and colour were like the satisfaction of a thirst to him; but it was only in the night . . . that he drew them out to enjoy their companionship . . . at night came his revelry: at night he closed his shutters, and made fast his doors, and drew forth his gold. He . . . felt their rounded outline between his thumb and fingers, and thought fondly of the guineas that were only half-earned by the work of the loom as if they had been unborn children. (65, 68, 70)

The pleasure that Eliot's miser takes in this illicit atmosphere ("only in the night"; "at night came his revelry"; "at night he closed his shutters, and made fast his doors") resembles a condensed catalog of sexual deviance—incest, of course—the "rounded outlines" that are the object of his nocturnal fondlings are the bodies of his own children "begotten by his labor"—but also the range of perversions that surrounds the "secret sin" of masturbation. Eliot's account of the revelry of this "pallid, undersized" man, isolated among full-bodied strangers, reads like a case study of the solitary practice and enervating consequences of self-abuse imagined by nineteenth-century sexology, consequences that range from bodily debilitation to homosexuality. Intimations of solitary and more than solitary vices are enfolded in the hard cash whose "rounded" and "resistant outlines" the miser fondles, outlines and "faces" not only "his own," but also *like* his own.[2] The miser's self-love suggests one that dares not speak its name, a love whose definition is glimpsed in the shadow of Sodom (whose eponymic reputation was as active in the nineteenth century as it is now) that hovers over "the City of Destruction" from which the miser is saved when the gold is replaced by the girl:

> In old days there were angels who came and took men by the hand and led them away from the city of destruction. We see no white-winged angels now. But yet men are led away from threatening destruction: a hand is put into theirs, which leads them forth gently towards a calm and bright land, so that they look no more backward; and the hand may be a little child's. (190–91)[3]

What is remarkable about *Silas Marner*'s propaganda campaign on behalf of familial propriety is less the lengths that Eliot goes to in its prosecution, or even the alarming shapes that threaten it, than the deficiency indicated by the very need for such a campaign in the first place. Her frank efforts to propagate a preference for family ties, or, more to my point here, her efforts to propagate an aversion for other kinds of congress, mark a loosening in *Silas Marner* of the quieter methods by which these things are usually inculcated in her fiction, a loosening whose promiscuous consequences verge on the regions of perversity, a loosening that I will eventually return to as a crisis of capital.

2

The appearance of impropriety that clings to the miser's fondlings is an affront to rules of proper bodily conduct, or more precisely, of proper bodily *contact*, a flouting of restrictions imposed by a not-just Victorian standard of propriety on the body's intercourse with others, a challenge to the frequently informal bylaws charged with the work of regulating

103

sexual relations. Often dwelling outside the annals of official or even explicit dictates, inhabiting instead "the seemingly most insignificant details of *dress*, *bearing*, physical and verbal *manners*," the rules of bodily propriety are easiest to observe in their breach:[4] like the sudden realization of speed limits prompted by the sound of a siren, proper distances between bodies in and beyond the Eliot novel are typically measured by what happens when those that should not, get too close, when intercourse between a man and woman who are not married, or between a man and another man, exceeds correct or normal bounds: full-scale scandal explodes when Maggie Tulliver spends the night with Stephen Guest and when Arthur Donnithorne does more than that with Hetty Sorrel. A scandal as intense as these is concentrated in the parlor where Dorothea Casaubon

> saw, in the terrible illumination of a certainty which filled up all outlines, something which made her pause motionless, without self-possession enough to speak.
>
> Seated with his back towards her on a sofa which stood against the wall on a line with the door by which she had entered, she saw Will Ladislaw: close by him and turned towards him with a flushed tearfulness which gave a new brilliancy to her face sat Rosamond, her bonnet hanging back, while Will leaning towards her clasped both her hands in his and spoke with a low-toned fervour. (*MM* 355)

A fear of scenes like this one is present whenever bodies that should not engage in such intercourse are left alone in the Eliot novel. "The terrible illumination of a certainty which filled up all outlines" (*MM* 634) confirms a suspicion admitted earlier, when Dorothea "found herself thinking with some wonder that Will Ladislaw was passing his time with Mrs Lydgate in her husband's absence" (*MM* 355), a suspicion like the one marked by the eyebrows raised when the otherwise impeccable Daniel Deronda spends too much time alone with Gwendolen: "After a moment's silence, in which Sir Hugo looked at a letter without reading it, he said, 'I hope you are not playing with fire, Dan—you understand me'" (*DD* 389).

The rumor of impropriety that Sir Hugo and Dorothea Casaubon detect is not confined to unchaperoned intercourse between unmarried men and women. It attends as well the closeted interviews between men, such as those between Fred Vincy and Peter Featherstone, who "would not begin the dialogue till the door had been closed" (*MM* 89). Mary

Garth suspects that such "loitering" costs Vincy his "manly independence" (*MM* 213); a perhaps related suspicion is cast by the "peculiar twinkle" in the eye of the old man: "When Fred came in the old man eyed him with a peculiar twinkle, which the younger had often had reason to interpret as pride in the satisfactory details of his appearance" (*MM* 89).

And if the strictures governing body contact in Eliot are made visible by their violation, their intensity is made vivid by all the care that she takes to prevent their appearance in the first place. The conduct book she keeps of the private interviews between Will Ladislaw and Dorothea Casaubon labors to demonstrate that no such scene as that between Will and Rosamond occurs when *these* bodies gather: "She gave her hand for a moment, and then they went to sit down near the window, she on one settee and he on another opposite" (*MM* 442); "Will sat down opposite her at two yards' distance" (*MM* 298); "he was standing two yards from her with his mind full of contradictory desires and resolves" (*MM* 445); "she moved automatically towards her uncle's chair . . . and Will, after drawing it out a little for her, went a few paces off and stood opposite to her" (*MM* 514–15).

The eccentricity of all this detail widens if we consider that it is delivered to the reader, who is privy to these private interviews, and not, say, to Mrs. Cadwallader, who might suspect closer contact between Will and Dorothea from the other side of the closed door. It is as if Eliot worries that our suspicion is sleepless enough to imagine all the things she denies here going on in front of our faces, as if she worries we might speculate, unless we are told otherwise, that Dorothea gave Will her hand for much more than a moment, as if she worries we would surmise, without explicit indication to the contrary, that they stand or sit much less than two yards from one another, as if she worries we would suppose, except for her denial, that after drawing her chair, Will *does not* walk "a few paces off."

Eliot compulsively lodges such transistorized affidavits in the minutiae of interviews like these, little logbooks showing that bodies which may get too close to one another do not. Whatever Grandcourt sees when he surprises Deronda and his wife alone, Eliot takes pains to show that it is not what Dorothea sees when she comes across Will and Rosamond: "What he saw was Gwendolen's face . . . and Deronda standing three yards off" (*DD* 521); Grandcourt himself, when he is alone with Gwendolen prior to their engagement, is "about two yards distant"

(*DD* 255); even the somewhat ampler allowance of body contact allotted to a betrothed couple is carefully measured: before they are married, "[Lydgate] touched [Rosamond's] ear and a little bit of her neck under it with his lips" (*MM* 289).

Such precise accountings hold themselves accountable to a sense of propriety always on the lookout for three feet on the floor. If they sometimes seem to aspire to the condition of choreography, they are always bending over backward to maintain for the bodies that inhabit them a good reputation in the eyes of an unblinking monitor of proper conduct. As with the neurosis that seems to exaggerate but actually clarifies the ordeals of civility, Eliot's obsessive documentation of adherence to it reflects an endless demand that bodies keep their proper distance. That such documentation, while obsessive, is delivered without apparent thought, without any sign of conscious intent, makes the conformity of the Victorian novel to the rules of bodily propriety as automatic as our own. With as little visible resolve as what is disclosed in the straightening of a wrist or a walk, the duration of a handshake or the length, location, and depth of a kiss, the body everywhere bends to the rigors of propriety, the body not more at home in the fiction of the nineteenth century than among the ways we live now.

Conducted unconsciously, the task of enforcing the rules of bodily propriety draws upon the defensive industriousness we have been taught to associate with what is unconscious. Eliot's text develops an elaborate network of impediments that ensure the conformity that it elsewhere documents in detail, tying hands that shouldn't wander, turning into marble forms not allowed to embrace: "It was as if [Deronda] saw Gwendolen drowning while his limbs were bound" (*DD* 389); "it had seemed to [Will Ladislaw] as if they were like two creatures slowly turning to marble in each other's presence, while their hearts were conscious and their eyes were yearning" (*MM* 444).

The measures that Eliot's text takes to prevent illicit intercourse do not merely isolate the proscribed body; they do not merely restrain the hand or the lips that would touch it. Such shapes are not simply fettered and distanced; they are entirely altered or even annulled as the meticulous labors of prohibition are aided by the miracles of metamorphosis. The pressure of propriety has alchemical powers: Eliot substantiates her efforts to deny anything scandalous about the intimacy between Ladislaw and Dorothea and between Gwendolen and Deronda by converting the body forbidden to the grasp into an object that one can see but not touch. Grandcourt may rest assured that his wife has avoided the extremities of adultery, not only because Deronda is "three yards off" from her, but also, and more important, because she is less a body capable of receiving the licentious grasp than a painting capable of compelling the admiring eye.[5] "What he saw was Gwendolen's face of anguish framed black like a nun's, and Deronda standing three yards off from her with a look of sorrow" (*DD* 521). Dorothea feels "helpless" to manifest her affection for Will because "her hands had been tied from making up to him for any unfairness in his lot." But even if they were not tied, Dorothea would not lay her hands on Will anyway, since all she wants to do is to look at him: "Her hands had been tied from making up to him for any unfairness in his lot. But her soul thirsted to see him" (*MM* 440). Eliot underwrites the distance she interposes between bodies that shouldn't touch by casting the relation between them as the two-dimensional communion of spectacle and audience, or the body that should not be "grasped" is evacuated altogether:

> The feeling Deronda endured in these moments he afterward called horrible. Words seemed to have no more rescue in them than if he had been beholding a vessel in peril of wreck—the poor ship with its many-lived anguish beaten by the inescapable storm. How could he grasp the long-growing process of this young creature's wretchedness . . . ? (*DD* 521)

Unchaperoned communion between a married woman and an unmarried man is defined here as a kind of communication that excludes any hands-on contact; as if that isn't enough, what can't actually be grasped anyway is then put at more than arm's length, put at a distance as remote as a vessel on stormy waters seen from the shore.

Eliot's accounts of the conduct of couples who shouldn't touch are sometimes less prolix than this, but seldom less busy abstracting the prohibited body. Casaubon, for example, abandoning his wife during their wedding tour, spends time "groping after his mouldy futilities" (*MM* 168) instead. That such precautions are doubled—physical or grammatical ("after") distances are imposed which separate bodies who are in any event incapable of touching or being touched—suggests a now-familiar anxiety: when it comes to physical intimacy, a single layer of protection may not be enough.

Indeed, when Eliot approaches the gathering of bodies where such anxiety is now most familiar, the number of sanctions that she imposes against illicit embrace constitute an otherwise impossible population explosion:

The two men, with as intense a consciousness as if they had been two undeclared lovers, felt themselves alone in the small gas-lit book-shop and turned face to face, each baring his head from an instinctive feeling that they wished to see each other fully. Mordecai came forward to lean his back against the wall hardly more than four feet off. I wish I could perpetuate those two faces, as Titian's "Tribute Money" has perpetuated two types presenting another sort of contrast. Imagine—we all of us can—the pathetic stamp of consumption with its brilliancy of glance to which the sharply-defined structure of features, reminding one of a forsaken temple, give already a far-off look as of one getting unwillingly out of reach; and imagine it on . . . the face of a man little above thirty, but with that age upon it which belongs to time lengthened by suffering, the hair and beard still black throwing out the yellow pallor of the skin, the difficult breathing giving more decided marking to the mobile nostril, the wasted yellow hands conspicuous on the folded arms: then give to the yearning consumptive glance something of the slowly dying mother's look when her one loved son visits her bedside, and the flickering power of gladness leaps out as she says, "My boy!"—for the sense of spiritual perpetuation in another resembles that maternal transference of self. (*DD* 424–25)

It is difficult to conceive how this passage could be more resourceful arresting the homosexual trajectory that it first sets in motion. As soon as the two men "with as intense a consciousness as if they had been two undeclared lovers" are about to touch (what else would follow now that they are finally alone, and face to face?), they are separated, first by four feet, and then again, more decisively, when one is placed "out of reach." The prospect of illicit intercourse prohibited by this double distance is subjected to a double dose of aversion therapy that makes both too much and too little of the proscribed body—too much to allow its appeal to survive ("the hair and beard still black throwing out the yellow pallor of the skin, the difficult breathing giving more decided marking to the mobile nostril"), too little to allow it to survive as a body at all ("the sharply-defined structure of features, reminding one of a forsaken temple"). The final touch of the dying mother gilds this lily of repression; whatever remains of a scene intense with the consciousness of two lovers who had felt themselves alone is fully dispelled by her appearance; it is as if the text has taken, *avant la lettre*, the shock methods advised by a sixties sex manual for deferring male orgasm ("Think of a turnoff—your grandfather; the war in Vietnam").

As we might well know, a prophylactic urge to deform or make disappear a body who appears susceptible to illicit embraces extends beyond the work of George Eliot. Leaving aside for a moment scenes and suppressions closer to home, recall the fate of *David Copperfield*'s Steerforth when the plaintive wish that his "Daisy" had a sister puts into play a desire that it barely misses mentioning for "Daisy" himself. The usual means by which homosexual appeal between men is covered over even as it is constituted nearly disappears here; the partition separating sanctioned from unsanctioned male intercourse in the exchange between Copperfield and Steerforth that we are about to encounter is narrowed to paper-thinness; the by-now well-known female figure through whom a desire between men is routinely routed reduced to a pretense as bare as the "friend" whose troubles are really our own:[6]

> The greater part of the guests had gone to bed as soon as the eating and drinking were over; and we, who had remained whispering and listening half-undressed, at last betook ourselves to bed, too.
>
> "Good night, young Copperfield," said Steerforth. "I'll take care of you."
>
> "You're very kind," I gratefully returned. "I am very much obliged to you."
>
> "You haven't got a sister, have you?" said Steerforth, yawning.
>
> "No," I answered.
>
> "That's a pity," said Steerforth. "If you had one, I should think she would have been a pretty, timid, little, bright-eyed sort of girl. I should have liked to know her. Good night young Copperfield."
>
> "Good night, sir," I replied.
>
> I thought of him very much after I went to bed, and raised myself, I recollect, to look where he lay in the moonlight, with his handsome face turned up, and his head reclining easily on his arm.

And again, just as the possibility of illicit bodily contact gains point, the body vaporizes:

> He was a person of great power in my eyes; that was, of course, the reason of my mind running on him. No veiled future dimly glanced upon him in the moonbeams. There was no shadowy picture of his footsteps, in the garden that I dreamed of walking in all night.[7]

Where is Steerforth in the moonlit thoughts of the boy who admires "his handsome face turned up, and his head reclining easily on his arm" with an intensity given everything but a name? While the landscape of David's dreamwork is pervaded by this "person of great power," his body is no-where to be found there: "No veiled future [even] dimly glanced upon him"; "there was no shadowy picture [even] of his footsteps."

The line of causalities we have been tracing in the work of Eliot and Dickens extends beyond the limits of the Victorian novel. According to Eve Kosofsky Sedgwick's revisionist history, the inclination to conceal the male body freighted with homoerotic potential takes on the global force of a systematic campaign in the war against figuration waged by several generations of literary modernism; in the urge toward abstrac-tion that marks modernism, the strategy of preemptive disappearance through which the likes of Steerforth, Mordecai, and Dorian Gray are disembodied expands to become the general form of a comprehensive literary imperative. And here I quote Sedgwick:

> Insofar as there is a case to be made that the modernist impulse toward abstraction in the first place owes an incalculable part of its energy precisely to turn-of-the-century male homo/heterosexual definitional panic—and such a case is certainly there for the making, in at any rate literary history from Wilde to Hopkins to James to Proust to Conrad to Eliot to Pound to Joyce to Hemingway to Faulkner to Stevens—to that extent the "figuration" that had to be abjected from modernist self-reflexive abstraction was not the figuration of just *any* body, the figura-tion of figurality itself, but, rather, that represented in a very particular body, the desired male body.[8]

The classic story of an absconded body that Sedgwick updates here ex-hibits a distinct opposition between power and its victims, a Manichae-ism implicit in any myth or hypothesis of repression, whether its culprit is a jealous god or the pressure of a homophobic propriety. On one side there is the body; on the other, a conspiracy to conceal the body. Dis-placed by plants or planets, or by nonfigurative literary landscapes on which nobody, and especially not the proscribed physique, can be seen, the censored body is set against the repressive forces that hide it. If the ruses of propriety that I have been assessing so far cast the prohibited body out of sight, they stop short of infecting that body. Thus the Fou-cauldian formation that Sedgwick elsewhere discovers, a "gay male rhet-oric . . . already marked and structured and indeed necessitated by the historical shapes of homophobia" (165), may be contrasted with the concealed corpus that she disinters in the passage I quoted before, the body abstracted by a homophobia concerned only to repress, rather than to constitute or contaminate it, the body that thus retains an illicit purity even when it is spirited away.[9]

It would be imprudent, if not simply impossible, to deny the enduring and practically pervasive vitality of the urge to hide this body. The habit of abstraction that stretches beyond the Victorian novel and beyond literary modernism into most contemporary spheres of representation introjects, and thus preempts, the efforts of an external censor to expunge the body seemingly ready to offer or to receive the wrong kind of touch. Bodies not transformed by the artful wands of sublimation are subject instead to the blunter interventions of a Mrs. Grundy or a Jesse Helms.

But even side by side with the perennial effort to censor the proscribed body, the forces of propriety are conducted as well, and sometimes even better, through other, more invasive operations; when these forces do not dissolve and displace the body that seems capable of inviting or offering the wrong kind of touch, they take up residence there. The forces of propriety infiltrate the physique they decline to erase, as anybody knows who has escaped the demand for concealment only to feel in its place a sense of unease never quite overcome. It is this deeper collaboration between propriety and the endangered and dangerous body that I turn to now.

3

The boundaries of propriety are felt along the pulse: no less than the novels they inhabit, the body in Eliot appears to absorb the rules governing its conduct. If Eliot's text takes and gives notice of these rules in the spectacle of their violation or in the immense and minute stratagems it enlists for avoiding this spectacle, the body situated there registers the demands of propriety in the form of sensations and perturbations that arise when they are transgressed, sensations and perturbations as slight and decisive as the usually barely noticeable aches and pangs and tics that mark our own fear that we have erred from the rigors of the social order. Well before Adam Bede punishes Arthur Donnithorne for what he does with Hetty Sorrel, even as "his arm is stealing round her waist," Donnithorne feels the consequence of this act in the form of a vague but decisive unease: "Already Arthur was uncomfortable. He took his arm from Hetty's waist."[10] When, during his courtship with Gwendolen, Grandcourt exceeds even slightly the "limit of an amorous homage"

("One day indeed . . . he had kissed not her cheek but her neck a little below her ear"), she suffers distress: "Gwendolen, taken by surprise, had started up with a marked agitation which made him rise too" (*DD* 275).

Such discomfort and agitation are most visible when they attend the scene in Eliot that comes closest to asserting an illicit desire between men, the nervous drama of intimacy between Daniel Deronda and Mordecai that I have already touched upon. Just as the rules regarding bodily propriety are observed in the Eliot novel only when they are violated or in danger of being violated, the homosexuality that never quite surfaces as an explicit theme is embodied in a homophobic unease—the aversion inspired by Mordecai's "spasmodic grasps" (*DD* 487), "eager clasps" (*DD* 433), his "thin hand pressing [Deronda's] arm tightly" (*DD* 327): "Deronda coloured deeply, not liking the grasp" (*DD* 327); "Daniel [rose], with a habitual shrinking which made him remove his hand from Mordecai's" (*DD* 429).

Deronda's aversion desists only when the hands that Mordecai lays on him are disembodied; only when the clutch of Mordecai's fingers gives way to the "clutch of his thought" (*DD* 411); "a yearning need which had acted as a beseeching grasp"; a "tenacious certainty" that acts as "a subduing influence" on Deronda (*DD* 431). This sublimating tide reaches its height near the end of the novel when the press of the flesh that everywhere marks the intercourse between Deronda and Mordecai is cast as the mere expression of a metaphysical communion, safely routed through a female vessel: "The two men clasped hands with a movement that seemed part of the flash from Mordecai's eyes, and passed through Mirah like an electric shock" (*DD* 640).

The discomfort that such abstraction works to attenuate arises again in the "strongly resistant feeling" Deronda experiences when, at the synagogue, while he is "moving away with the rest," the body next to his unexpectedly breaks rank:

> He had bowed to his civil neighbour and was moving away with the rest—when he felt a hand on his arm, and turning with the rather unpleasant sensation which this abrupt sort of claim is apt to bring, he saw close to him the white bearded face of that neighbour. . . . Deronda had a strongly resistant feeling: he was inclined to shake off hastily the touch on his arm. (*DD* 311)

Deronda's civil neighbor is excessively so: the very remarking of his closeness marks it as too close, just as the abruptness of the hand on the arm betrays its deviation from normality. While we are probably inclined to dismiss Deronda's reaction to this as an instance of his often-re-marked priggishness, Eliot casts the "strongly resistant feeling" that arises for him in the face of even an apparently slight eccentricity from the conventions of bodily contact as a general response: *everyone* is apt to experience the "unpleasant sensation which this abrupt sort of claim . . . bring[s]." Eliot's penchant for declaring the situation of particular characters a universal condition is quite superfluous here: Deronda's sensations are merely the socially arranged reflex of the male subject when another man's body gets even a little too close, the male subject, it hardly seems necessary to say, not limited to the literature of the nine-teenth century.

After all, such responses couldn't be more familiar; they are common to everybody who is subject to a sense of bodily propriety no less active here and now than in the Victorian novel. The discomfort that Arthur Donnithorne experiences and the agitation that Gwendolen Harleth suffers are well known to anyone for whom sexual guilt or sexual threat has ever taken form as a feeling of unease; the aversion that Deronda senses when others of his own gender get too close is the experience of every man, in and beyond the Victorian novel.

But if these allergic reactions are only too familiar to a culture of un-ease as much our own as George Eliot's, their precise identity, and the nature of the subject who suffers them, remains mysterious. Eliot's pro-file of these things is too shapeless to conform to a simple physical or physiological definition, too vague to be solely attributed to the body. ("Already Arthur was uncomfortable"; "Gwendolen, taken by surprise, had started up with a marked agitation which made him rise too"; "De-ronda [did] not lik[e] the grasp"; "Daniel [rose], with a habitual shrink-ing which made him remove his hand from Mordecai's"; "Deronda had a strongly resistant feeling.")

It's not exactly or exclusively the body that shrinks habitually from a deviant touch or is agitated or uneasy when a hand or a kiss steals past a limit at once informal and excruciatingly precise. Nor is it exactly or exclusively the mind that suffers these things. The amorphous expe-rience marked by Donnithorne's discomfort, or Gwendolen Harleth's agitation, or Deronda's "strongly resistant feeling" or "rather unpleas-ant sensation" is confined to the province of neither the body nor the spirit.

To be subject to such ambiguous unease is to be a subject for whom the labors of apprehension and the pains of the body are utterly con-fused, a subject for whom the disturbances of the mind melt into the diseases of the flesh, a subject for whom the laws of propriety make two kinds of sense, a subject in whom a spirit that knows the laws and a body that feels them are so mingled that they cannot be distinguished. The subject susceptible to the forces of propriety whom these forces are able not merely to repress but to infiltrate, consists not of a body or a mind; it is instead a hybrid formation where these strains are crossed.

This conflation of abstract consciousness and bodily experience drives to the point of identity terms usually more loosely linked by an atmosphere of analogical suffering especially dense in the Eliot novel. What, for the very fact of its frequency, might pass for the usual, even inevitable analogy between physical and metaphysical disease takes on the consistency of an anagogical system in the world of George Eliot: "Notions and scruples were like split needles, making one afraid of treading, or sitting down, or even eating" (*MM* 18); "Will's reproaches . . . were still like a knife-wound within her" (*MM* 652); "this man's speech was like a sharp knife-edge drawn across her skin" (*DD* 512); "his words had the power of thumbscrews and the cold touch of the rack" (*DD* 582); "he's got a tongue like a sharp blade, Bartle has" (*AB* 213); "as soon as he took up any antagonism, though only in thought, he seemed to himself, like the Sabine warriors in the memorable story—with nothing to meet his spear but flesh of his flesh" (*DD* 307).

The subject of mental duress in Eliot is everywhere haunted by a body in pain, a phantom partner in suffering such as the one that Maggie Tulliver devises to represent all her struggles:

> A large wooden doll . . . which once stared with the roundest of eyes above the reddest of cheeks . . . was now entirely defaced by a long career of vicarious suffering. Three nails driven into the head commemorated as many crises in Maggie's nine years of earthly struggle.[11]

Such chambers of torture can be found anywhere in an Eliot novel; a parallel universe of physical unease, ranging from medieval extremities of agony to blander or subtler discomforts, hovers, like the roar on the other side of silence, over the ordinary world of abstract distress. The rhyme between apprehension and sensation, "knowledge" and "feeling," praised by two Eliots as the touch of the poet,[12] is not the mark of any single class of consciousness; it is a universal facility in the works of at least one of them. An honor-destroying revelation "enters like a stab into Bulstrode's soul" (*MM* 568) and is felt as much by his wife, who "needed time to get used to her maimed consciousness, her poor lopped life" (*MM* 614). Less apocalyptic apprehensions are no less linked to bodily trauma; even the normal disappointments of maturity are shadowed by the ruin or amputation of the body: "Life must be taken up on a lower stage of expectation, as it is by men who have lost their limbs" (*MM* 533).

What such comparisons offer with one hand they take away with the other. It is of course in the nature of analogies to confirm the difference between the terms they draw together, and the correspondence that Eliot habitually proposes between physical and metaphysical pain is no exception to this rule. Such analogies work like the endlessly newsworthy discovery that psychological stress takes tolls on the body ranging from colds to cancer, like the less positivist intuition that the slings and arrows of outrageous fortune or the push and shove of daily life have more than figurative force, like any incidental lifting of what one theorist of the body's pains calls "a Cartesian censorship," a "rigorously enforced separation in the subject between psyche and soma."[13] The usual link between abstract and bodily discomfort in the Eliot novel depends upon and reinforces their fundamental distinction.

But in the subject who suffers for even the smallest sins of impropriety, all differences between mind and body are abolished; in this conventional character, the partial unity of psyche and soma accomplished by analogy gives way to the more astonishing achievement of incarnation. If this character calls to mind a supernatural conjunction, a word made flesh, it may be as usefully classed among the more mundane annals of social reproduction. The subject whose ambiguous sensations enforce the rules of propriety in the Eliot novel joins ranks with an array of others anatomized by contemporary investigations of the body's social construction, the figure, for example, whom Pierre Bourdieu describes as the embodiment of the metaphysical imperatives of a social order:

> If all societies . . . that seek to produce a new man through a process of "deculturation" and "reculturation" set such store on the seemingly most insignificant details of *dress*, *bearing*, physical and verbal *manners*, the reason is that, treating the body as a memory, they entrust to it in abbreviated and practical, i.e. mnemonic, form the fundamental principles of the arbitrary content of the culture. The principles em-bodied in this way are placed beyond the grasp of consciousness, values given body, *made* body by the transubstantiation achieved by the hidden persuasion of an implicit pedagogy, capable of instilling a whole cosmology, an ethic, a metaphysic, a political philosophy, through injunctions as insignificant as "stand up straight" or "don't hold your knife in your left hand."[14]

115

The incorporation that Bourdieu describes here, the figure in whom the "fundamental principles of the arbitrary content of the culture" are "made body," is like the subject that a range of feminist theory has in mind when it construes the sexed body as the incarnation of an abstract gender system; it is like the subject at the center of Michel Foucault's investigations of modern power formations, a body who incorporates the discursive marks of the disciplinary procedures and sexual identifications that inhabit the brave new world he charted.[15]

These various subjects of social discipline are too various to admit any effort to lock them into step with one another. The embodiments featured in recent speculations on the social uses of the flesh cannot be neatly collated with the figure who is subject to the rules of bodily propriety in the Eliot novel: the terms of mind and body that are drawn together in these figures are too disparate to allow it. But both the body made to bear the discipline of a social order and the composite subject made to feel it are beings at the same time carnal and abstract. In every case, the subject's capacity to absorb the various definitions and demands of the social order depends upon his capacity to be at once spirit and flesh.

It is this conjunction, the one that characterizes the subject of social discipline in and beyond the Eliot novel, that is undone by the miser's passion in *Silas Marner*. I turn now to consider how the miser's commerce eludes both the pattern of abstraction that prevents violations of the rules of proper conduct in the Eliot novel from appearing in the first place and, more crucially, the subjective aversions that typically arrest them when they do. I turn now to consider how the miser's fondlings, his revelry with the "bright faces" and "rounded outlines" of his coins, supply both an object and a subject capable of resisting what normally thwarts the illicit embrace and how the love of money serves the interests of perversity by baffling all the forces of propriety.

4

In *Silas Marner*, the miser's love is the means of indemnifying the subject and object of deviant passion against the sense of aversion that normally attacks it and the force of abstraction that normally eclipses it. In the miser's love, the hybrid subject who is vulnerable to the demands of propriety in the Eliot novel dissolves, and when it does, the social discipline made solid in such a subject melts into air. The character capable of sensations at once physical and metaphysical is dismantled by the miser's devotions and replaced by a subject entirely corporeal, one therefore immune to the amorphous sensations by which the body's correct conduct is enforced.[16]

To chart the avenue of simplification by which Silas Marner eludes the dictates of propriety, we need first to notice how the miser and his money work to form one another. In a condensed version of the labor theory of value, according to which the commodity's worth reflects the bodily effort reposited there, both *Silas Marner* and Silas Marner cast the miser's money as the reproduction of his own body—either his children or his clones: "The crowns and half crowns that were his own earnings" are "begotten by his labour (70)"; "he . . . thought fondly of the guineas that were only half earned . . . as if they had been unborn children" (70); "it was pleasant to feel them in his palm, and look at their bright faces, which were all his own" (65).[17] And conversely, if the money is the reembodiment of Silas Marner, he, in turn, is the reembodiment of the coins: "Like all objects to which a man devotes himself, they had fashioned him into correspondence with themselves" (92).

The body with which Silas Marner comes to correspond is invulnerable to sensations of pain or bitterness or unease for the simple reason that it is invulnerable to any sensation at all. "Hidden away from the daylight," the gold is "deaf to the sound of birds"—as well as to every other sound; it "starts at no human tones" (184)—nor does it start at any other tones. Like Dolly Winthrop's child who "looked like a cherubic head untroubled with a body" (139), the coins are untroubled by a body, or, more exactly, untroubled *as* a body, by any sensation—not only those arranged by "the sound of birds" or "human tones," but also the more complex ones that cause Silas Marner's fiancée to "shrink" with aversion from him: "Didn't the gold [just] lie there after all?" (93).

Silas Marner identifies with the coins he adores by assuming a version of their insensibility: "The gold had asked that he should sit weaving longer and longer deafened and blinded more and more to all things except the monotony of his loom and the repetition of his web" (184). Just as his money is cast in his image, the miser himself is re-formed in the shape of his money. This reciprocity replenishes the relation between laborer and artifact whose diminution Elaine Scarry mourns as the cost of "the capitalist economic system":

> The large all-embracing artifact, the capitalist economic system, is itself generated out of smaller artifacts that continually disappear and reappear in new forms: out of the bodies of women and men, material

117

objects emerge; out of material objects commodities emerge; out of commodities, money emerges; out of money, capital emerges. . . . In its final as in its first form, the artifact is a projection of the human body; but in its final form, unlike its first, it does not refer back to the human body because in each subsequent phase it has taken as the thing to which it refers only that form of the artifact immediately preceding its own appearance. . . . The overall work of its successive forms is to steadily extend the first consequence (capital is, like the solitary pair of eyeglasses or any other made object, the projected form of bodily labor and needs) and to steadily contract the second: each new phase enables the line of reciprocity to pull back further and further from its human source until the growing space between the artifact and its creator is at last too great to be spanned either in fact or in an act of perception.[18]

All that Elaine Scarry declares lost on the path of abstraction arranged by the "capitalist economic system" is restored in the miser's world, congested with the full complement of two-way traffic between the laborer and even his most attenuated issue. The miser's money returns to him not only in an "act of perception," but also "in fact": No less than the body that wears them is transformed by eyeglasses, Silas Marner is changed by the money he adores.

But there is more than one difference between the eyes given sight by the artifact of labor that Scarry mentions and the miser made blind by the tokens of his work. While the artifact that Scarry envisions reforms the body, the coins effect the complex character we have noticed before, the character in whom the body and mind are merged. The miser's blindness is not of the eyes: when Silas Marner takes on the insensitivity of the coins, he is stripped not of his senses, but rather of his sensibility. Here, the composite character who experiences the aversions that arise when the rules of propriety are violated is reduced to the miser's "shrunk[en]" (69) frame. A distinction that the novel admits in the difference it stages between natural and adopted fathers appears again when the miser's physical senses are parted from metaphysical ones; the doors of perception are cleansed of their abstract dimensions, extricated from the faculties of metaphysical apprehension with which they are usually entangled.

And as the miser falls to sleep in spirit, he awakens to a utopian erotics of pure sensation: "Now when all purpose was gone," the "habit of looking towards the gold and grasping it with a sense of fulfilled effort made a loam that was deep enough for the seeds of desire" (65). The "thrill of satisfaction" that the coin provides consists entirely of its "touch"; the miser's "phantasm of delight," drawn down from the realm of spirit where phantasms dwell normally, is now no more than the simple matter of "feeling" (68) and "handling" (129) the coins. Just as his life "narrows and hardens into a mere pulsation of desire and satisfaction that has no relation to any other being" (68), his "revelry" (70) of "immediate sensation" (68) has no relation to anything other than itself.

The miser, now an entirely sensuous being, is no longer a subject in whom the physical and the metaphysical are merged, the subject who is subject to the rules of propriety in and beyond the Eliot novel. A body wholly body, the miser is ready to enjoy the revelry that we noticed earlier, a perverse pleasure that would sicken others, and again, not just in the work of George Eliot. And if the influence that the coins exert on the miser renders him immune to the disciplinary aversions to which subjects are generally susceptible when they cross the borders of propriety, the reciprocal projection, which casts the coins as the issue of his body, renders it such a transgression in the first place. *Silas Marner*'s fairy-tale telling of the labor theory of value reverses the defensive bias by which bodies that shouldn't be touched are abstracted in the Eliot novel. That the "rounded outlines" the miser handles and feels are those of a body is the outcome of a current countering the general tide in the Eliot novel, a tide that draws the desire to touch back into the safety zone of disembodiment.

All of this perversity is dispelled when the miser's money disappears and his stepdaughter arrives on the scene. The therapy administered by the girl who replaces the coins reattaches the sensibility from which the miser is freed by the ministrations of the gold, "reawakening his senses with her fresh life": "As her life unfolded, his soul, long stupefied in a cold narrow prison, was unfolding too, and trembling gradually into full consciousness" (184, 185). Through his life as a father, Silas Marner's feelings are freighted now with metaphysical capacities; his delight in Eppie consists not simply in sensing her, but also in sensing the need to sense her: "I'd got to feel the need o' your looks and your voice and the touch o' your little fingers" (226). The abstractions of sensibility are affianced again to the physical senses when Silas Marner leaves off the love of gold and takes up the love of a girl. While the miser "feels" the gold in one sense only, the "senses" that are reawakened under the influence of Eppie are doubled, consisting not only of the capacity to apprehend matters of the senses, "the old winter-flies that came crawling forth in the early spring sunshine" (184), but also of the capacity to apprehend things metaphysical.

While the miser's revelry accompanies the divorce of his senses from abstract sensations, the weaver's respectability emerges with their remarriage; with this remarriage, the normal, normalized subject reappears. Silas Marner forsakes the eccentricities that rendered him a stranger in a strange land; "making himself as clean and tidy as he could" (183), he enrolls in a remedial course on familial respectability, entrusting both Eppie and himself to the dictates of chapel and hearth. "He had no distinct idea about the baptism and the churchgoing, except that Dolly had said it was for the good of the child" (183–84).[19]

Silas Marner's "new self" (201) is subject to a restraint quite absent in the old one, a reluctance to lay a hand on the body that he considers his "own child." The sense of propriety that slept while the miser fondled "rounded outlines" "all his own" returns here with a force sufficient to make even the prospect of wholesome body contact unbearable to him. Silas Marner is compelled to refuse the measures that Dolly Winthrop or George Eliot name, or fail to name, with a compunction matching his own: "Dolly Winthrop told him that punishment was good for Eppie, and as for rearing a child without making it tingle a little in soft and safe places now and then, it was not to be done" (185). The squeamishness manifested in a circumlocution that avoids even the mention of touching the body appears again when the miser declares that he must avoid any discipline that involves its practice: "'She'd take it all for fun,' he observed to Dolly, 'if I didn't hurt her, and that I can't do'" (188). After its brief interruption, the regime that enforces the restrictions imposed on touching proceeds now with no end in sight. The laying on of hands that was to "frighten [Eppie] off touching things", is eschewed for other methods to prevent such contact: Silas Marner, subject now to the restraint he is charged with imposing, must do what Eliot does with the measures of distance she takes to prevent the illicit touch of bodies, "must do what [he] can to keep 'em out of her way" (188).

Silas Marner takes decisive steps to seal off the channel that enabled the miser's exemption from propriety, steps to stop the intercourse of gold and bodies that produced both a physique able to avert those sensations and a physique that would allow them to be incited in the first place. The novel puts an end to the intercourse between gold and bodies that makes Silas Marner a purely sensuous subject and that casts the money he hoards as a shape susceptible to an illicit touch. At first, the miser's "blurred vision" confuses the gold with the girl, "but instead of hard coin with the familiar resisting outline, his fingers encountered soft warm curls" (167). The correction that takes form here as a tactile proof

120

that even the dissolute miser can understand is expanded as the novel progresses, driving a deeper difference between the gold and the body: not only is the weaver wrong to suppose that the gold is the girl, he is wrong to imagine that the gold becomes the girl. A story of metamorphosis, in which gold is transformed into a body and is thus able to preserve its character in translation, gives way to a story of substitution, in which the body merely replaces the gold. This fading of the rumor of transubstantiation takes place in Silas Marner's mind: at first, "he could have only said that the child was come instead of the gold—that the gold had turned into the child" (180); finally, though, he succumbs to the force of disenchantment, teaching Eppie that he "had taken her golden curls for his lost guineas" (204). While this account puts both the models of metamorphosis and substitution into play, it consigns the first to the miser's own dubious perceptions—his taking gold curls for lost guineas is almost indistinguishable from mistaking gold curls for lost guineas—while granting the second the irresistible power of fact.

Eliot works overtime to discredit the affiliation between money and bodies; the differences that the miser encounters are the subject of a homily that we encountered before:

> The gold had kept his thoughts in an ever-repeated circle, leading to nothing beyond itself; but Eppie was an object compacted of changes and hopes that forced his thoughts onward . . . to the new things that would come with the coming years, when [she] would have learned to understand how her father Silas cared for her. . . . The gold had asked that he should sit weaving longer and longer, deafened and blinded more and more to all things except the monotony of his loom and the repetition of his web; but Eppie called him away from his weaving, and made him think all its pauses a holiday, re-awakening his senses with her fresh life. (184)

With an economy we are entitled to expect from a novelist whose words, no matter how many, always do as much as they can, Eliot encourages family values and discourages the condition that disrupted them. However briefly—others have labored even more consistently to sustain a familial, familiar regime of propriety whose profits and losses have only accrued with the passing of time.

❋ Afterword ❋

Truly it was impossible to dissociate her presence from
all those wretched hankerings after money and gentility that had
disturbed my boyhood—from all those ill-regulated aspirations
that had first made me ashamed of home . . . from all those
visions that had raised her face in the glowing fire, struck it out
of the iron on the anvil, extracted it from the darkness of night
to look in at the wooden window of the forge and flit away.

(*Charles Dickens*, Great Expectations)

AGAIN AND AGAIN, the story is the same: nothing gold can stay. Like the inconstant woman in whom it is typically engrossed, the figure who rises from "the glowing fire" or "from the darkness of night," only to disappear again, the luminous shapes of capital advertised in and beyond the Victorian novel disappoint expectations of endurance, great and small.[1] Slipping through the fingers of even the tightest grip, capital is more like a volatile gas than a solid property: As often as night follows day, or what is repressed returns, the miser's hoard is taken from him; the gains of merchant and adventurers go the way they came; the palace of affluence melts into air.

And like the fateful desire for a cruel mistress where it often convenes, the "wretched hankering after money," and the silver-plated "gentility" that money buys, is an "ill-regulated aspiration" that makes its victim ashamed of home and home ashamed of him. For if the forms of capital audited by the Victorian novel baffle the hope for the stability entrusted in a woman called home, they also encourage and accommodate passions that have no place there. In the ambiguous undulations of currency and accounting books, in the vivid shapes vended by streetwalker and marriage broker, in the capital of bodies and the bodies of capital, are figures that blast the protocols of propriety that the Victorian novel teaches as the virtue of home, just as surely as they annul the dream of stable estate that it helped to place among home's comforts.

Such hazards couldn't be farther removed from a promise of capital commonly entertained in the century before the Victorian novel. For in the love of money, Albert O. Hirschman declares in his digest of "arguments for capitalism before its triumph," "men were expected or assumed to be steadfast, single-minded, and methodical, in total contrast to the stereotyped behavior of men who are buffeted and blinded by their passions."[2] Hirschman tells us that the calmness that Hume, Montesquieu, and Dr. Johnson associated with making money was often hailed as an indispensable instrument by theorists anxious to sustain social security. Moderate and moderating, the love of money was applauded as a means to counteract and contain less tractable, more unruly passions, ready at the drop of a handkerchief or a zipper to disrupt public order and decency.

This conception persists through the nineteenth century to the present day. It endures in the character of the bloodless capitalist made famous by Weber and Marx, the one-dimensional man whose rich appetites and aspirations are reduced to the colorless principle of monetary gain. But as we know, and not just from the Victorian novel, capital declines as often as performs the work of discipline or distraction attributed to it by its admirers and enemies. By the time a much-longed-for kiss from a cold and glittering girl is "given to the coarse common boy" of *Great Expectations* "as a piece of money might have been" (121), capital is identified with and as a too-fascinating passion, as much as it is hailed or condemned as the means by which such passions are stilled, stifled, or sublimated. By the time of the miser's orgy in *Silas Marner*, the love of money is cast as one that surpasses the limits of church and state, as much as it is apprehended as a force that would discourage such perversity.

A more reliable agent of propriety is found elsewhere in the Victorian novel, in the devotions inspired by the domestic monitor whose durability there as property we have already appreciated. Removed at once from the vicissitudes of passion and interest, the homebody stationed at the closing scenes of the Victorian novel shimmers with the assurance of two securities that capital fails to supply:

> And now, as I close my task, subduing my desire to linger yet . . . one face, shining on me like a Heavenly light by which I see all other objects, is above them and beyond them all. And that remains.
>
> I turn my head, and see it, in its beautiful serenity, beside me. My lamp burns low, and I have written far into the night; but the dear presence, without which I were nothing, bears me company.
>
> O Agnes, O my soul, so may thy face be by me when I close my life indeed; so may I, when realities are melting from me, like the shadows which I now dismiss, still find thee near me, pointing upward![3]

123

Armed with everlasting light, the angel of the house, no less than "my soul" with which she merges, answers the prayer for enduring property, the prayer whose call is heard across and beyond the regions of the Victorian novel. But she does more than that: subduing the desire to linger later in the night, encouraging steady and punctual effort, the woman conscripted at home is assigned the duties of propriety that capital can no longer be relied upon to discharge. The angel of the house is the still point in an age of capital whose perpetual crises show no sign of waning, the place of peace where all ravishings, except those she pays for herself, are put to rest.

* *Notes* *

CHAPTER ONE
INTRODUCTION

1. E. J. Hobsbawm, *The Age of Capital: 1848–1875* (New York: New American Library, 1975, 1979). Subsequent citations of Hobsbawm refer to this edition.

2. See, for example, Karl Marx, *Capital*, vol. 1, trans. Ben Fowkes (1867; reprint, New York: Vintage Books, 1977); Immanuel Wallerstein, *Historical Capitalism* (London: Verso, 1983).

3. This is the period generally characterized as the industrial phase of capitalism, which saw the exponential expansion of capital-labor relations and the successful struggles of laissez-faire partisans to end state regulation of markets (the repeal of the Corn Laws and Navigation Acts). See Hobsbawm, *The Age of Capital*; Asa Briggs, *The Age of Improvement 1783–1867* (London: Longmans, Green, 1959); David Thomson, *England in the Nineteenth Century, 1815–1914* (New York: Penguin Books, 1950, 1978); Marx, *Capital*.

4. Thomas Carlyle, *Past and Present*, ed. Edwin Mims (1843; reprint, New York: Charles Scribner's Sons, 1918), 196.

5. Edward George Earle Lytton Bulwer-Lytton, Baron, *England and the English* (New York: J. & J. Harper, 1833), 1:86.

6. Wallerstein, *Historical Capitalism*, 10.

7. See, for example, Karl Marx, *The German Ideology*, ed. C. J. Arthur (New York: International Publishers, 1970); Georg Lukács, *History and Class Consciousness: Studies in Marxist Dialectics*, trans. Rodney Livingstone (Cambridge, Mass.: MIT Press, 1971), 83–222; Theodor W. Adorno, *Prisms*, trans. Samuel Weber and Shirley Weber (Cambridge, Mass.: MIT Press, 1981); Frederic Jameson, *The Political Unconscious* (Ithaca: Cornell University Press, 1981).

8. William Makepeace Thackeray, *Vanity Fair*, (1847–48; reprint, New York: Oxford University Press, 1983), 201. All subsequent citations of *Vanity Fair* refer to this edition.

9. Barbara Lee Smith Bodichon, *A Brief Summary in Plain English of the Most Important Laws of England Concerning Women* (London, 1854).

10. The shock induced by the female commodity is a perennial one; for a compact summary of ancient, medieval, and modern apprehensions of this figure, see Catherine Gallagher, "George Eliot and *Daniel Deronda*: The Prostitute and the Jewish Question," in *Sex, Politics and Science in the Nineteenth-Century Novel: Selected Papers from the English Institute 1983–1984*, ed. Ruth Bernard Yeazell (Baltimore: Johns Hopkins University Press, 1986), 39–62.

Animosity toward the buying and selling of women expresses itself both in the testimony of common sense and in a range of nineteenth- and twentieth-century feminist-Marxist theory, which condemn heterosexual relations and the market economy or both by pointing to the exchange of women as their definitive instance. See, for example, Karl Marx and Friedrich Engels, "The Communist Manifesto," *Collected Works*, vol. 6 (New York: International Publishers, 1970); Emma Goldman, "The Traffic in Women," in *The Traffic in Women and Other Essays on Feminism* (New York: Times Change Press, 1971); A. Bebel, *Women under Socialism*, trans. D. De Leon (New York: Schocken Books, 1971); Sheila Rowbotham, *Woman's Consciousness, Man's World* (New York: Penguin, 1973); Gayle Rubin, "The Traffic in Women: Notes Toward a Political Economy of Sex," in Rayna Reiter, ed., *Towards an Anthropology of Women* (New York: Monthly Review Press, 1975), 157–210.

11. Charles Dickens, *Dombey and Son* (1848; reprint, New York: Penguin Books, 1984), 473. All subsequent citations of *Dombey and Son* (hereafter *DS*) refer to this edition.

12. The literature of and about the separate spheres is, of course, vast. For its Victorian expression, see John Ruskin, "Sesame and Lilies," in *Works* 18 (1923), 122; and Sarah Ellis, *The Women of England* (1839); *The Wives of England, Their Relative Duties, Domestic Influence, and Social Obligations* (1843). Leonore Davidoff and Catherine Hall extensively document the practical and ideological separation of the domestic and the marketplace in the late eighteenth and nineteenth centuries. *Family Fortunes: Men and Women of the English Middle Class, 1780–1850* (London: Hutchinson, 1987). See especially 149–316. For general discussions of the Victorian cult of separate spheres, see Françoise Basch, *Relative Creatures: Victorian Women in Society and the Novel*, tr. Anthony Rudolf (New York: Schocken Books, 1974); Martha Vicinus, ed., *A Widening Sphere: Changing Roles of Victorian Women* (Bloomington: Indiana University Press, 1977); Elizabeth K. Helsinger, Robin Lauterback Sheets, and William Veeder, *The Woman Question: Society and Literature in Britain and America, 1837–1883*, 3 vols. (New York: Garland Publishing, 1983); Mary P. Ryan, *Women in Public: Between Banners and Ballots, 1825–1880* (Baltimore: Johns Hopkins University Press, 1990). The feminine bias of the domestic realm confirmed in the Victorian period has alarmed some critics, sometimes for alarming reasons. See Christopher Lasch, *Haven in a Heartless World: The Family Besieged* (New York: Basic Books, 1977). For a discussion of Lasch's account as patriarchal nostalgia, as well as a general survey of theoretical assessments of separate-sphere ideology, see Michele Barrett and Mary McIntosh, *The Anti-Social Family* (New York: Verso, 1982, 1991). On the contemporary effects of separate-sphere ideology, see Karen V. Hansen and Ilene J. Philipson, eds. *Women, Class and the Feminist Imagination: A Socialist-Feminist Reader* (Philadelphia: Temple University Press, 1990).

13. Mid-Victorian advocates of the separate spheres never seemed to tire of telling how the home where woman is made to dwell becomes her. Container and contained converge in a famous garden coronation, where an illustrious propagandist of women's estate makes the homebody shimmer with glamour:

This is the true nature of home—it is the place of Peace . . . so far as it is a sacred place, a vestal temple, a temple of the hearth watched over by House-hold Gods, before whose faces none may come but those whom they can receive with love,—so far as it is this . . . so far it vindicates the name, and fulfils the praise, of Home. . . . And wherever a true wife comes, this home is always round her. The stars only may be over her head; the glowworm in the night-cold grass may be the only fire at her foot; but home is yet wherever she is; and for a noble woman it stretches far round her, better than ceiled with cedar, or painted with vermilion, shedding its quiet light far, for who else were homeless. . . . This, then, I believe to be . . . the woman's true place and power. (John Ruskin, "Of Queen's Gardens," in "Sesame and Lilies," *Works* 18:122)

The vision of domesticity that Ruskin publishes resolves into a single form as the multiple faces of the household gods merge into one, as the garden she inhabits merges with the figure of the queen. If woman is angel of the house, home is the paradise of devotion within and about her; dwelling where she does, the range of the home is measured not by the walls of any house, but rather by the extent of her reflection. On the conception of home as emanation of woman, the "outermost garment of her soul," see Ellis, *The Women of England*.

14. "He was immensely pleased with his young lady; Madame Merle had made him a present of incalculable value" (Henry James, *Portrait of a Lady* [1881; reprint, New York: Penguin Books, 1984], 401).

15. Walter Benn Michaels, "Romance and Real Estate," in *The Gold Standard and the Logic of Naturalism* (Berkeley: University of California Press, 1987), 104. Like Michaels's account of nineteenth-century American literature, my assessment of the Victorian novel describes the loss of marketable property as not merely possible, but virtually inevitable. But while Michaels assumes the slide from the possibility to the inevitability of this loss, I want to delineate how the Victorian novel imagines the details of this confusion of potential with necessary alienation. Moreover, while Michaels is concerned with the circulation of property in the marketplace, I will be concerned with the circulation of property more generally.

16. For readings of love and property in the Victorian novel which cast these terms as simply opposed to one another, see Monroe Engel, *The Maturity of Dickens* (Cambridge, Mass.: Harvard University Press, 1959); Ross H. Dabney, *Love and Property in the Novels of Dickens* (Berkeley: University of California Press, 1967).

17. Walter E. Houghton, *The Victorian Frame of Mind* (New Haven: Yale University Press, 1957), 61. Such stories were especially harrowing in the nineteenth century where, as Houghton remarks, there "was no such thing as limited liability" (61).

18. "Homologies . . . between the circulation of land sold and bought, the circulation of 'throats' 'lent' and 'returned' (murder and vengeance), and the circulation of women given and received, that is between the different forms of capital and the corresponding modes of circulation oblige us to abandon the dichotomy of the economic and the non-economic which stands in the way of seeing the science of economic practices as a particular case a general science of the economy of practices, capable of treating all practices, including those purporting to be disinterested or gratuitous, and hence non-economic, as economic practices" (Pierre Bourdieu, *Outline of a Theory of Practice*, trans. Richard Nice [Cambridge: Cambridge University Press, 1977], 183). On the ideological division of economic and noneconomic modes of circulation, see Karl Polanyi, *The Great Transformation: The Political and Economic Origins of Our Time* (Boston: Beacon Press, 1944), especially 71; Jürgen Habermas, *The Structural Transformation of the Public Sphere: An Inquiry into a Category of Bourgeois Society*, trans. Thomas Burger (1962; reprint, Cambridge, Mass.: MIT Press, 1989).

19. Charles Dickens, *Little Dorrit* (1857; reprint, New York: Oxford University Press, 1982). Subsequent citations of *Little Dorrit* refer to this edition.

20. Marcel Mauss, *The Gift: Forms and Functions of Exchange in Archaic Societies*, (trans. Ian Cunnison) (1925; reprint, New York: W. W. Norton, 1967). For a critique of the economism of Mauss's essay, see Georges Bataille, "The Notion of Expenditure," in *Visions of Excess: Selected Writings, 1927–1939*, trans. Alan Stoekl (Minneapolis: University of Minnesota Press, 1985), 116–29.

21. "The ownership of a thing cannot be looked upon as complete without the power of bestowing it, at death or during life, at the owner's pleasure: and all the reasons, which recommend that private property should exist, recommend *pro tanto* this extension of it" (John Stuart Mill, *Principles of Political Economy*, ed. Donald Winch [1848; reprint, New York: Penguin, 1970], 376).

22. "A market economy demands that property be freely transferable so that it can pass from hand to hand" (P. S. Attiyah, *The Rise and Fall of Freedom of Contract* [New York: Oxford University Press, 1979], 87). While Attiyah's point refers specifically to economic capital, it is no less applicable to other forms of capital, since they too are defined by their portability. For different statements of the point that Attiyah makes here, see Marx, *Capital*, vol. 1, chap. 2, 178–79, and C. B. Macpherson, *Property: Mainstream and Critical Positions* (Toronto: University of Toronto Press, 1978), 8.

23. Dickens, *Little Dorrit*, 681.

24. Victorian feminists concerned with reforming married women's property law noted that the abbreviation or abrogation of married women's rights to own property was concomitant with the conversion of such women into the property

of their husbands. See Susan Kingsley Kent, *Sex and Suffrage in Britain, 1860–1914* (Princeton: Princeton University Press, 1987), 88; Mary Lyndon Shanley, *Feminism, Marriage, and the Law in Victorian England, 1850–1895* (Princeton: Princeton University Press, 1989), 156–88.

25. John Stuart Mill, *The Subjection of Women*, introduction by Wendall Robert Carr (1869; reprint, Cambridge, Mass.: MIT Press, 1970, 1988), 11–12, 28, 31–32. See also Karl Marx: "*Marriage* . . . is incontestably a form of *exclusive private property*" ("Private Property and Communism," in *Early Writings*, trans. T. B. Bottomore [1844; reprint, New York: McGraw-Hill, 1963], 153).

26. See also William Thompson, *Appeal of One Half of the Human Race*: "Each man yokes a woman to his establishment, and calls it a *contract*. Audacious falsehood! A contract! where are any of the attributes of contracts, of equal and just contracts, to be found in this transaction? A contract implies the voluntary assent of both the contracting parties. Can even both the parties, man and woman, by agreement alter the terms, as to *indissolubility* and *inequality* of this pretended contract? No" (*Appeal of One Half of the Human Race, Women, against the Pretensions of the Other Half, Men, to Retain Them in Political, and Thence in Civil and Domestic Slavery*, ed. Richard Pankhurst [1825; reprint, New York: Virago Press, 1983]).

27. Bodichon, "A Brief Summary of the Laws Concerning Women."

28. Kent, *Sex and Suffrage in Britain*, 85.

29. Virginia Woolf, *Three Guineas* (London: Chatto & Windus, 1938).

30. See, for example, Lisa Vogel, "The Contested Domain: A Note on the Family in the Transition to Capitalism," *Marxist Perpectives* 1 (Spring 1978), cited by Judith Lowder Newton, *Women, Power, and Subversion: Social Strategies in British Fiction, 1778–1860* (Athens: University of Georgia Press, 1981), 18.

31. Mary Poovey, *Uneven Developments: The Ideological Work of Gender in Mid-Victorian England* (Chicago: University of Chicago Press, 1988), 10; Nancy Armstrong, *Desire and Domestic Fiction: A Political History of the Novel* (New York: Oxford University Press, 1987). These accounts are schooled in a tradition of Marxist and post-Marxist theory generally associated with the work of Louis Althusser and Michel Foucault, work that suspects regions of the social order usually cast as sites of resistance to the forces of the law, or capitalism, as stations that collaborate with these forces by means of their very difference from them. Louis Althusser, "Ideology and Ideological State Apparatuses (Notes Towards an Investigation)," in *Lenin and Philosophy and Other Essays*, trans. Ben Brewster (New York: Monthly Review Press, 1971); Michel Foucault, *The History of Sexuality*, vol. 1, *An Introduction*, trans. Robert Hurley (New York: Vintage Books, 1980). For literary registrations of power's differential operations, see D. A. Miller, *The Novel and the Police* (Berkeley: University of California Press, 1988).

32. Thus Nancy Armstrong notes that in the eighteenth- and nineteenth-century novel, "competing class interests are . . . represented as a struggle between the sexes that can be completely resolved in terms of the sexual contract." My argument approaches Poovey's when, in her study of the controversy surrounding married women's rights during the nineteenth century, she notes that "one of the functions of the opposition between the private, feminized sphere and the masculine sphere of work outside the home, was to mitigate the effects of the alienation of market relations" (77). But Poovey's concern for the economic function of the "private, feminized sphere" is restricted to the suspension of market exigencies that it effects. According to her analysis, the split within the self who sells his labor, a split between the subject who sells and the subject who is sold, is rewritten at home as the difference between the husband who owns property and a wife who represents it. For Poovey, the economy of the domestic consists of stilling the self division that the market provokes. I am arguing that the suspension of market economics (and the economics of circulation in general) that takes place in what Victorian publicists of the separate spheres call home also enables another economic relation, the one marked by Little Dorrit's nuptial vow.

33. Dabney, *Love and Property*, 120. The opposition that Dabney assumes here between "economic advantage" and "affection" informs a wide range of criticism of both Dickens and Eliot: While the pursuit of economic advantage crowds out inner desires according to most critical accounts of it, those accounts themselves often move in the opposite direction, reading economic events and conditions as metaphors or occasions for psychological struggles. For this tendency among Dickens's critics, see, for example, Steven Marcus, *Dickens from Pickwick to Dombey* (New York: W. W. Norton, 1965); Grahame Smith, *Dickens, Money and Society* (Berkeley: University of California Press, 1968); John Lucas, *The Melancholy Man* (Totowa, N.J.: Harvester Press, 1980). This bias operates as well in the work of Eliot's critics, who often either celebrate or condemn her famous perspicacity about affairs of the heart and mind as a turn away from affairs of business. See, for example, Barbara Hardy's account of *Silas Marner*, which reads the text as a psychological rather than an economic account of the miser (*Particularities: Readings in George Eliot* [London: Peter Owen Press, 1982], 13); William Myers criticizes the Eliot who "habitually psychologizes social fact" and ignores "concrete factors in social and economic life" ("George Eliot: Politics and Personality," in *Literature and Politics in the Nineteenth Century*, ed. John Lucas [London: Methuen, 1971], 105–29). In *The Country and the City*, Raymond Williams argues that Eliot's isolation of individual psychology from social pressures, including economic ones, recapitulates the general reification that characterizes nineteenth-century England (New York: Oxford University Press, 1973). In *Social Figures: George Eliot, Social History, and Literary Representation*, Daniel Cottom argues that the realm of affect in Eliot provides the site for the imaginary resolution of social and economic contradictions

and conflicts. While this argument articulates a relation between the economic and the psychic, it also confirms their difference (Minneapolis: University of Minnesota Press, 1987).

34. George Eliot, *Daniel Deronda* (1876; reprint, New York: Penguin Books, 1988), 481. Hereafter *DD* in text.

35. Roland Barthes, *S/Z*, trans. Richard Miller (New York: Hill & Wang, 1974), 216.

36. I refer here to a tradition of Marxist criticism discussed and exemplified by Terry Eagleton and Frederic Jameson. See, for instance, Terry Eagleton, *Criticism and Ideology* (New York: New Left Books, 1976); Frederic Jameson, *The Political Unconscious* (Ithaca: Cornell University Press, 1984).

37. Marx, *Capital* 1:138.

38. Alfred Sohn-Rethel, *Intellectual and Manual Labour: A Critique of Epistemology*, trans. Martin Sohn-Rethel (London: Macmillan Press, 1978), 25.

39. For a different account of the ghostliness of the angel of the house, see Alexander Welsh, *The City of Dickens* (Oxford: Clarendon Press, 1971), 180–95.

40. Albert O. Hirschman, *The Passions and the Interests: Political Arguments for Capitalism Before Its Triumph* (Princeton: Princeton University Press, 1977), 41. Subsequent citations of Hirschman refer to this edition.

41. Charles Dickens, *Our Mutual Friend* (1865; reprint, New York: Penguin, 1985), 177.

CHAPTER TWO
DOMESTIC SECURITIES

1. Jean-Jacques Rousseau, *Discourse on the Origin and Foundation of Inequality*, ed. and trans. Roger D. Masters and Judith R. Masters (New York: St. Martin's Press, 1975), 141–42.

2. R. H. Tawney, *The Acquisitive Society* (London: Harvester Press, 1921), 51.

3. Dickens, *Little Dorrit* 347.

4. For another account of the significance of debt for *Little Dorrit*, see F. R. Leavis and Q. D. Leavis, "Dickens and Blake," *Dickens the Novelist* (Edinburgh: R. & R. Clark, 1970), 213–76, especially 221–25. In "Secret Pockets and Secret Breasts: *Little Dorrit* and the Commercial Scandals of the Fifties," Barbara Weiss places the novel's anxiety about debt in a historical context (*Dickens Studies Annual* 10 [1982]: 67–76).

5. See, for example, Claude Lévi-Strauss, "Introduction a l'oeuvre de Marcel Mauss," in *Sociologie et Anthropologie* (Paris: PUF, 1950), xxxviii.

6. Georges Bataille, "The Notion of Expenditure," in *Visions of Excess: Selected Writings, 1927–1939*, trans. Allan Stoekl (Minneapolis: University of Minnesota Press, 1985), 116–29; Pierre Bourdieu, "The Objective Limits of Objectivism," in *Outline of a Theory of Practice*, 1–9.

7. Annette B. Weiner, *Inalienable Possessions: The Paradox of Keeping while Giving* (Berkeley: University of California Press, 1992), 30.

8. Rosalind Coward, *Patriarchal Precedents* (London: Routledge & Kegan Paul, 1983), 151–52.

9. Marx, *Capital* 1:277.

10. In her comparison of the anxious toil of Bradley Headstone with the careless enfranchisement of Eugene Wrayburn ("Homophobia, Misogyny and Capital: The Example of *Our Mutual Friend*," in *Between Men* (New York: Columbia University Press, 1985), Eve Kosofsky Sedgwick casts the visibility of the effort of acquisition as a sign of economic marginality. Like Miss Wade, Bradley Headstone is allotted only a visible and "perverse" means for getting: "Sphincter domination is Bradley Headstone's only mode for grappling for the power that is continually flowing away from him" (169).

CHAPTER THREE
FOR YOUR EYES ONLY

1. This passage parodies, by rendering explicit, the covert task of the nineteenth-century explorer-writers whom Mary Louise Pratt discusses in "Scratches on the Face of the Country; or, What Mr. Barrow Saw in the Land of the Bushmen." The work of information gathering that engaged these explorer-writers "is the project whereby, to use Daniel Defert's terms, Europe 'takes consciousness of itself . . . as a planetary process rather than [as] a region of the world.' This nineteenth-century exploration writing rejoins two planetary processes that had been ideologically sundered: the expansion of the knowledge edifice of natural history and the expansion of the capitalist world system." (*Critical Inquiry* [Autumn 1985]: 125).

2. For a discussion of capitalist apologies for imperialism during the Victorian period, see C. C. Eldridge, *England's Mission: The Imperial Idea in the Age of Gladstone and Disraeli, 1868–80* (London: Macmillan, 1973); *Victorian Imperialism* (London: Macmillan, 1978). For a summary of some Marxist accounts of imperialism, see Anthony Brewer, *Marxist Theories of Imperialism, A Critical Survey* (London: New Left Books, 1978).

3. This motif is repeated in *The Mystery of Edwin Drood* (London: Oxford, 1972), in its account of the cozy private quarters of Mr. Tartar: "There was a seagoing air upon the whole effect, so delightfully complete, that . . . the whole concern might have bowled away gallantly with all on board" (189). All subsequent citations of *Drood* refer to this edition.

4. Williams, "The New Metropolis," in *The Country and the City.*

5. This position is first elaborated by K. Marx, *Early Manuscripts*, trans. T. B. Bottomore (New York: McGraw-Hill, 1964). For a lucid summary of this affiliation, see Macpherson's "The Meaning of Property," in *Property.*

6. In *The Imagination of Charles Dickens* (New York: Random House, 1962) A.O.J. Cockshut notices that Dombey's "pride" consists of his implicit claim of

aristocratic identity (101). I am suggesting that this pride not only expresses his pretense of aristocratic station, but also enables this pretense. The haughty incommunicativeness of the capitalist is not only a sign of his assumption of lordship, but also its condition. Cockshut observes that Dombey's pretense depends on the dearth of other aristocratic claims in the novel (100). I want to claim that this pretense depends, more radically, on the absence of others per se: Dombey can only "lord . . . *alone*" (my emphasis). The identification of the secret as the mystique of specifically aristocratic property appears again in *Bleak House*, in Dickens's account of the secrets that the lawyer Tulkinghorn hoards: "There are noble Mausoleums rooted for centuries in retired glades of parks . . . which perhaps hold fewer noble secrets than walk abroad among men, shut up in the breast of Mr. Tulkinghorn . . . steward of . . . legal mysteries" (London: Oxford University Press, 1951), 11–12. Subsequent citations of *Bleak House* refer to this edition.

7. For another reading of *Dombey*'s problem with money, one that casts it as the agent and emblem of moral defects, see F. R. Leavis and Q. D. Leavis, "The First Major Novel: *Dombey and Son*," in *Dickens the Novelist* (Edinburgh: R. & R. Clark, 1970), 1–30.

8. Bourdieu, *Outline of a Theory of Practice*.

9. The novel's conception of capital as a form of communication accords with the postmodern economics charted by Jean Baudrillard, in *Critique of the Political Economy of the Sign* (Saint Louis: Telos Press, 1979). Baudrillard argues that the various instances of economic value that inhabit capitalism are all elements in the functioning of the sign.

10. "Everywhere, the commodity teemed with signification—so much so that Marx, in his famous chapter in *Capital* on commodity fetishism, had to shift metaphors every few sentences to do justice to its ubiquity and plasticity as a form of representation; . . . Capitalism was now consolidating its hold over England not only economically, but semiotically" (Thomas Richards, *The Commodity Culture of Victorian England* [Stanford: Stanford University Press, 1990], 2–3); Jennifer Wicke, *Advertising Fictions: Literature, Advertisement, Social Reading* (New York: Columbia University Press, 1988).

11. Georg Simmel describes the unique accessibility of money, its inability to harbor any secret or surprise: "We know more about money than about any other object because there is nothing to know about money and so it cannot hide anything from us. It is a thing absolutely lacking in qualities and therefore cannot, as can even the most pitiful object, conceal within itself any surprises or disappointments" (Georg Simmel, *The Philosophy of Money*, trans. Tom Bottomore and David Frisby [Boston: Routledge & Kegan Paul, 1978], 303). If according to Simmel money cannot conceal, according to *Dombey and Son* it cannot be concealed.

12. Various critics and historians described the novel as the center of the commodification of literary production and reception, and Dickens is often cited as the first example of this new system. See, for example, Ian Watt, *The Rise of the*

Novel (Berkeley: University of California Press, 1957); Normon Feltes, *Modes of Production of Victorian Novels* (Toronto: University of Toronto Press, 1988). For an account of Dickens's efforts to retain control over access to the capital of his novels, see Alexander Welsh, *From Copyright to Copperfield* (Cambridge, Mass.: Harvard University Press, 1987).

13. In "Secret Subjects, Open Secrets," in *The Novel and the Police*, D. A. Miller describes the merging of the character of the novel and the subject of power. Considering the scene in *David Copperfield* where David is compelled to wear a humiliating sign on his back, Miller writes: "As the subject of readerly perusal unable to *look back*, David assumes the very ontology of a character in fiction" (32). A similar conflation takes place in *Dombey and Son*, when Dombey cannot avoid, because he cannot perceive, the ubiquitous eyes of the world ("Mr. Dombey and the World", in *DS*). And if the circumstance of the fictional character describes the subject inscribed in a social order represented by the panopticon, this circumstance describes as well the self-canceling character of property that falls under the sign of capital.

14. Jacques Donzelot, *The Policing of Families*, trans. Robert Hurley (New York: Random House, 1979).

15. Foucault, *The History of Sexuality*, 32.

16. In *The Imagination of Charles Dickens*, Cockshut criticizes the treatment of the prostitute in *Dombey and Son*: "He is guilty here of a failing very common in novelists of strong convictions—he is making a character do the author's work for him by commenting (as if from above) upon her own personality" (105). The feature that Cockshut complains of here might be read as a reflection of the tendency of the signs of sexuality to converge with the narrative of the novel.

17. Edward Said, *Orientalism* (New York: Random House, 1978), 39.

18. For accounts of the Victorian construction of the Orient, see, for example, Patrick Brantlinger, "Victorians and Africans: The Creation of the Dark Continent," *Critical Inquiry* (Autumn 1985); *Rule of Darkness: British Literature and Imperialism, 1830–1914* (Ithaca: Cornell University Press, 1988).

19. Charles Dickens, "The Noble Savage," in *Household Words* (London: Bradbury and Evans, 1850–1859), 477–501.

20. It is the bodily reserve displayed in passages like this, I suspect, that has tempted readers of *Dombey and Son* to speculate that Dombey and Edith never have sex. See Alan Horseman, preface to the Oxford edition of *Dombey and Son*.

21. See *The Oxford English Dictionary*'s history of the term.

22. Christine Bolt, "Race and the Victorians," in *British Imperialism in the Nineteenth Century*, ed. C. C. Eldridge (New York: Macmillan, 1984), 129.

23. A provocative instance of the invocation of the Oriental as a means of embodying sexuality appears in Jean Baudrillard's analysis of the erotic fetish object as the bodily site on which an abstract sexuality, "bound up in a general stereotype of *models of beauty* . . . the final disqualification of the body, its subjection to a discipline, the total circulation of signs," is reinscribed: "Tattoos, stretched lips, the bound feet of Chinese women, eyeshadow, rouge, hair re-

moval, mascara, or bracelets, collars, objects, jewelry, accessories: anything will serve to rewrite the cultural order on the body; and it is this that takes on the effect of beauty." Baudrillard locates the erotic in the *embodiment* of the abstract, while Dickens, I am arguing, identifies the erotic as abstract, but in either case, whether it be Dickens's registration of the embodiment of sexuality or Baudrillard's notice of the work of embodiment that is sexuality, the Oriental body is constitutive. "Anything will serve to rewrite the cultural order on the body," but Baudrillard's own account begins with "tattos, stretched lips, the bound feet of Chinese women" ("Fetishism and Ideology," in *Critique*, 94). A similarly ethnically ordered list appears shortly later: "Levi-Strauss has already spoken of this erotic bodily attraction among the Caduveo and the Maori, of those bodies 'completely covered by arabesques of a perverse subtlety,' and of 'something deliciously provocative'" ("Fetishism," 95). My point, of course, is not that the order of Baudrillard's list accurately represents the actual history of the embodiment of sexuality, but rather that Baudrillard's own conception of this embodiment is founded on the Oriental body.

24. For discussions of the discursive force of the Oriental sexual slave market in the nineteenth century, see Brantlinger, "Victorians and Africans"; Sander L. Gilman, "Black Bodies, White Bodies: Toward an Iconography of Female Sexuality in Late Nineteenth Century Art, Medicine, and Literature," *Critical Inquiry* (Autumn 1985).

25. Edward William Lane, *The Arabian Nights' Entertainments* (London: Bradbury and Evans, 1838).

26. "The Thousand and One Humbugs," in *Household Words*, 440–51.

27. Ibid. See the contents of David Copperfield's library and Dickens's letters to Forster about his childhood readings. Charles Dickens, *Selected Letters* (Oxford: Oxford University Press, 1966), 274–78; 317–23. The significance for Dickens of the Arabian Nights as a form of exhibition is amplified by Deborah A. Thomas's report that Dickens was profoundly influenced by them as a model for storytelling, seeking to emulate their form in his first fictional efforts. See Deborah A. Thomas, *Dickens and the Short Story* (Philadelphia: University of Pennsylvania Press, 1982).

28. See the second entry for *awake* in *The Oxford English Dictionary*: "To rise from a state resembling sleep, such as death" (*The Compact Edition of the Oxford English Dictionary*, vol. 1 [Oxford: Oxford University Press, 1971], 590–91.

Chapter Four
Daniel Deronda and the Afterlife of Ownership

1. Georg Simmel, *The Philosophy of Money*, trans. Tom Bottomore and Davis Frisby (Boston: Routledge & Kegan Paul, 1978), 304. All subsequent citations of Simmel refer to this work and this edition.

2. Charles A. Reich, "The New Property," in Macpherson, ed., *Property*,

180. The identification of possession as an arena of freedom has taken various shapes in the history of property theory. See Alan Ryan, *Property* (Minneapolis: University of Minnesota, 1987), for a summary of the most prominent strains of thought (liberal or neoliberal) that regard property as the instrument of the preservation of freedom. As Ryan suggests, this notion remains central to contemporary considerations of property. Roberto Mangabeira Unger notes that "there are still conservative publicists who see . . . the existing system of contract and property rights . . . as directly allied to the cause of freedom and even as part of the necessary definition of freedom itself" (*The Critical Legal Studies Movement* [(Cambridge, Mass.: Harvard University Press, 1983], 98).

3. Alan Ryan, *Property and Political Theory* (New York: Basil Blackwell, 1984), 230.

4. W. B. Friedman, "Changes in Property Relations," in *Transactions of the Third World Congress of Sociology* 1–2 (1956): 175.

5. Simmel's equation of property and power speaks for a wide tradition of property theory, a tradition that includes Locke and his neoliberal heirs, a tradition faded now into the ideological light of common day. But Simmel is specifically engaged here with Hegel's definition of the category. See Hegel, *Philosophy of Right*, trans. T. M. Knox (New York: Oxford University Press, 1967), 42.

6. On the historical heterogeneity of the category of possession, see also Karl Marx, "Introduction to a Critique of Political Economy," in *The German Ideology*, 124–51; and Paul Hirst's critique of Pashukanis in *On Law and Ideology* (London: Macmillan, 1979), 155. For a discussion of the tensions between duty-bound and absolute ownership, see J.G.A. Pocock, *The Machiavellian Moment: Florentine Political Thought and the Atlantic Republican Tradition* (Princeton: Princeton University Press, 1975).

7. Lawrence Stone, *An Open Elite?* (New York: Oxford University Press, 1986), 50–51. Stone and others advance various determinations to explain the sense of obligation that the ownership of estates entailed, most of which describe it as the ideological dimension of a strategy to retain aristocratic hegemony.

8. For the translation of inheritance into heredity, see Foucault, *History of Sexuality*. See also Gillian Beer, *Darwin's Plots*, for a discussion of the way Darwin's work was deployed to biologize inheritance. Gillian Beer, "George Eliot: *Daniel Deronda* and the Idea of a Future Life," *Darwin's Plots: Evolutionary Narrative in Darwin, George Eliot, and Nineteenth-Century Fiction* (Boston: Routledge & Kegan Paul, 1983).

9. It is appropriate that this duty consists of a nationalist project, since nationalism is closely tied to the idea of ownership I am considering here, the idea of ownership that defines the franchise as responsibility. See Ryan and Pocock for discussions of the alliance between nationalism and duty-bound possession (Ryan, *Property*; Pocock, *The Machiavellian Moment*). Gillian Beer notices the different ways that race and national culture are defined in the nineteenth century as forms of duty-bound possession (*Darwin's Plots*, 203–4).

10. See, for example, Thomas Carlyle, *Chartism* (London: J. Fraser, 1840); *Past and Present*, ed. Edwin Mims (1843; reprint, New York: Charles Scribner's Sons, 1918).

11. Elizabeth Fox-Genovese and Eugene Genovese, *Fruits of Merchant Capital* (New York: Oxford University Press, 1985), 344.

12. Marx, *Capital* 1:178. A consensus embracing Marxist and liberal property theory concurs with Marx here. The right of possession, which is "not only the right to enjoy or use" but also, and more importantly, "a right to dispose of, to exchange, to alienate," applies, according to C. B. Macpherson, to "property in the *bourgeois* sense" (Macpherson, *Property*). But see also Attiyah, *The Rise and Fall of Freedom of Contract*.

13. Attiyah, *Rise and Fall*, 87.

14. As cited in ibid., 93.

15. Bodichon, "A Brief Summary of the Laws Concerning Women," 17.

16. For a general review of the remarkable philosophical contortions that American law performed in an effort to maintain this distinction, and its ultimate failure to do so, see Fox-Genovese and Genovese's "Jurisprudence and Property Relations," in *Fruits of Merchant Capital*. The sense that proprietorial prerogative necessarily included "the power to bestow" is conversely confirmed by the insistence frequently heard in the second half of the nineteenth century that people cannot be property precisely because they *cannot* be bestowed. Here, for example, is the religious socialist Thomas Hill Green addressing the Leicester Liberal Association in 1880: "We are all now agreed that men cannot rightly be the property of men. . . . A contract by which any one agreed for a certain consideration to become the slave of another we should reckon a void contract. Here, then, is a limitation upon the freedom of contract which we all recognize as rightful" (Thomas Hill Green, "Liberal Legislation and Freedom of Contract," excerpted in Elizabeth Jay and Richard Jay, eds., *Critics of Capitalism* [New York: Cambridge University Press, 1986], 188).

17. Fox-Genovese and Genovese, "Physiocracy and Propertied Individualism," in *Fruits of Merchant Capital*, 277, 285.

18. George Eliot, *Middlemarch* (New York: Oxford University Press, 1988), 262. All subsequent references to this text (hereafter abbreviated as *MM*) refer to this edition.

19. This dilemma, according to which the exercise of the utmost power of possession is one with its end, is registered, in different terms, in the paradoxical character of the contract. On one hand, the contract, during the nineteenth century, was the record and ritual of absolute proprietorial prerogative. Claire Dalton notes that "contractual obligation was seen . . . into the latter part of the nineteenth century . . . to arise from the will of the individual" (Claire Dalton, "An Essay in the Deconstruction of Contract Doctrine," in Sanford Levinson, ed., *Interpreting Law and Literature* [Evanston, Ill.: Northwestern University Press, 1988], 285–318). On the other hand, this mirror and means of absolute proprietorial prerogative are also the means by which the owner contracts his will.

20. This is what D. A. Miller calls the "discontent" of "traditional" narrative: "In the last analysis, what discontents the traditional novel is its own condition of possibility. For the production of narrative—what we called the narratable—is possible only within a logic of insufficiency, disequilibrium, and deferral" (Miller, *Narrative and Its Discontents*, 265). See also Barthes, *S/Z*.

21. See, for example, Shlomith Rimmon-Kenan, *Narrative Fiction: Contemporary Poetics* (New York: Methuen, 1983), 1–5; Miller, *Narrative and Its Discontents*; Peter Brooks, *Reading for the Plot* (New York: Random House, 1984).

22. Neil Hertz, "Some Words in George Eliot: Nullify, Neutral, Numb, Number," in *Languages of the Unsayable: The Play of Negativity in Literature and Literary Theory*, ed. Sanford Budick and Wolfgang Iser (New York: Columbia University Press, 1989), 280–97. Hertz furnishes a very different account of Lapidoth's status as the site of a linguistic function, or dysfunction.

23. Marcel Mauss describes such a scenario in *The Gift*. Unless and until an offering is returned, the recipient dwells under the shadow of the donor's name. Marcel Mauss, *The Gift: Forms and Functions of Exchange in Archaic Exchange*, tr. Ian Cunnison (New York: W. W. Norton, 1967).

24. Orlando Patterson, *Slavery and Social Death* (Cambridge, Mass.: Harvard University Press, 1982), 30. All subsequent citations refer to this edition.

25. William Blackstone, quoted in Attiyah, *Rise and Fall*, 217.

26. Michel Foucault, *Discipline and Punish*, trans. Alan Sheridan (New York: Random House, 1979); and *The History of Sexuality*.

27. Foucault, *The History of Sexuality*, 138.

28. "The classic text is pensive: replete with meaning . . . it still seems to be keeping in reserve some ultimate meaning, one it does not express but whose place it keeps free and signifying . . . if the classic text has nothing more to say than what it says, at least it attempts to 'let it be understood' that it does not say everything. . . . Just as the pensiveness of a face signals that this head is heavy with unspoken language, so the (classic) text inscribes within its system of signs the signature of its plenitude: like the face, the text becomes *expressive* (let us say that it signifies expressivity). . . . At its discreet urging, we want to ask the classic text: What are you thinking about? But the text, wilier than all those who try to escape by answering *about nothing*, does not reply, giving meaning its last closure: suspension" (Barthes, *S/Z*, 216–17).

29. Foucault, *The History of Sexuality*, 89.

30. Miller, *Narrative and Its Discontents*, 179, 194. In *Reading for the Plot*, Peter Brooks casts these elements in the language of psychoanalysis, identifying the ambivalence of narrative telos with the aims and detours that constitute the death drive.

31. Beer, *Darwin's Plots*, 221, 227. For another account of the engendering of relations of domination, see Jessica Benjamin, *Bonds of Love: Psychoanalysis, Feminism, and the Problem of Domination* (New York: Random House, 1988).

CHAPTER FIVE
THE MISER'S TWO BODIES

1. George Eliot, *Silas Marner* (New York: Penguin Books, 1985), 181. All subsequent citations refer to this edition.

2. On the nineteenth-century construction of homosexuality as a desire defined by the similarity, even the identity, between its subject and object, as a construction that displaces the older notion of inversion, which involved no notion of similarity or sameness between these terms, see Jeffrey Weeks, *Coming Out: Homosexual Politics in Britain, from the Nineteenth Century to the Present* (New York: Quartet Books, 1979), 23–32. See also Eve Kosofsky Sedgwick's assessment of the current hegemony of this construction: "*homo-sexuality* . . . is now almost universally heard as referring to relations of *sexuality* between persons who are, because of their sex, more flatly and globally categorized as *the same*" (*The Epistemology of the Closet* [Berkeley: University of California Press, 1990], 158–59).

3. While "the City of Destruction" alludes most immediately to *Pilgrim's Progress*, behind that is Sodom. Louis Crompton surveys the ways in which the biblical account of Sodom and Gomorrah were invoked in the nineteenth century to define and wage war against homosexual activity (*Byron and Greek Love: Homophobia in Nineteenth-Century England* [Berkeley: University of California Press, 1985], 13–15, 258, 275–76, 278–79, 348). See also Sedgwick, *Epistemology of the Closet*, 127–28; Robert J. Corber, "Representing the 'Unspeakable': William Godwin and the Politics of Homophobia," *Journal of the History of Sexuality* 1, no. 1 (1990): 85–101; A. D. Harvey, "Prosecutions for Sodomy in England at the Beginning of the Nineteenth Century," *Historical Journal* 21 (1978): 939–48.

4. Bourdieu, *Outline of a Theory of Practice*, 94. This is not to say that such rules are exclusively implicit; they are grasped as well by the formal mechanisms of social power. For a discussion of nineteenth-century legal prosecution of homosexuality, see n. 3; for a potent contemporary example of the legal codification of homophobia, see the majority opinion of the Supreme Court in *Bowers v. Hardwick* (1986).

5. None of this denies the erotic investment of the visual that has concerned psychoanalytic theory. See Freud's discussions of scopophilia, *Three Essays on Sexuality* and "Instincts and Their Vicissitudes"; Laura Mulvey, "Visual Pleasure and Narrative Cinema," *Screen* 16, no. 3 (Autumn 1975): 6–18. My concern is to notice that the body's displacement by spectacle in the Eliot novel averts the hazards of impropriety, rather than averting the matter of sexuality altogether.

6. See Eve Kosofsky Sedgwick, *Between Men: English Literature and Male Homosocial Desire* (New York: Columbia University Press, 1985).

7. Charles Dickens, *David Copperfield* (New York: Penguin Books, 1985), 140.

8. Sedgwick, *Epistemology of the Closet*, 167.

9. For a critique of such accounts, see Foucault, "The Repressive Hypothesis," in *The History of Sexuality*, 15–49.

10. George Eliot, *Adam Bede* (New York: Penguin Books, 1982), 183. All subsequent citations of *Adam Bede* refer to this edition, hereafter abbreviated as *AB*.

11. George Eliot, *The Mill on the Floss* (New York: Penguin Books, 1980), 78–79. All subsequent citations of *The Mill on the Floss* refer to this edition.

12. "To be a poet is to have a soul so quick to discern that no shade of quality escapes it . . . a soul in which knowledge passes instantaneously into feeling, and feeling flashes back as a new organ of knowledge" (*MM* 183); T. S. Eliot, "The Metaphysical Poets," in *The Sacred Wood* (London: Faber & Faber, 1920).

13. D. A. Miller, "*Cage aux folles*: Sensation and Gender in Wilkie Collins's *The Woman in White*," in *The Novel and the Police*, 146–91.

14. Bourdieu, *Outline for a Theory of Practice*, 94.

15. For lucid critical accounts of feminist theorizations of sex as the incarnation of gender, see Diana Fuss, *Essentially Speaking* (New York: Routledge, 1989), 39–72; Judith Butler, *Gender Trouble* (New York: Routledge, 1990). Foucault, *Discipline and Punish* and *The History of Sexuality*. Such unifications of body and mind may be noticed at times to work like the analogies I have considered in the Eliot novel to maintain the distinction between these terms even as it remarks the suspension of that distinction. The embodiment of social principles may be read as an event, where what is fundamentally or primordially abstract is made flesh.

16. For other accounts of intercourse between sexuality and capital, see Michaels, "*Sister Carrie*'s Popular Economy" and "The Phenomenology of Contract," in *The Gold Standard and the Logic of Naturalism*, 29–58, 113–36.

17. The various permutations of the labor theory of value all involve complications that, even apart from the obvious reason for doing so, would reject the conception of the miser's money as his biological issue or his reincarnation. But in its deviation from the contemporary literature on the relation between the body and economic value, *Silas Marner* describes an important current within it. The condensation of the labor theory of value recorded in Eliot's text, the conception of the coins that the miser earns not as the abstract effect or measure of his work but rather as "unborn children," the confusion of the earnings that he "begets" by his labor as the issue begotten through another kind of labor, enacts a compulsion to incarnate that appears in a wide range of Victorian thought. Catherine Gallagher notes that the major political economists of the nineteenth century, as well as their critics, not only regarded labor as the source of wealth, but also, when calling for a recognition of the superior value of commodities that serve to replenish the body, "accord a privileged position to the commodities that are most easily turned back to flesh." The urge to restore the commodity to the body is, according to Gallagher, manifested as a more radical iden-

140

tification of these terms in *Our Mutual Friend*. Here, Gallagher argues, the commodity does not merely derive from and return to the body, but the commodity and the body are revealed to be the same thing. An analogous identification appears in *Silas Marner* when the miser casts his money in the shape of a body (Catherine Gallagher, "The Bio-Economics of *Our Mutual Friend*," in *Fragments of a History of the Human Body, Pt. 3* [New York: Zone Books, 1989], 344–65). For a survey of the history of the labor theory of value, see Maurice Dobb, *Theories of Value and Distribution since Adam Smith* (Cambridge and New York: Cambridge University Press, 1973).

18. Elaine Scarry, *The Body in Pain* (New York: Oxford University Press, 1985), 259–60. As Scarry acknowledges elsewhere in *The Body in Pain*, her reading of the Marxist scenario may be taken to literalize excessively the presence of the body of labor in the object of labor (245–46). To that extent, *The Body in Pain* participates in rather than merely describes the bias toward embodiment that Gallagher traces in a variety of nineteenth-century considerations of economic value, a bias we see as well in *Silas Marner*.

19. The story of Silas Marner's developing conformity to community standards is read more optimistically by Q. D. Leavis, who interprets the novel as a parable praising the virtues of a pastoral neighborliness, ruined by the advent of industrial capitalism. While Leavis regards *Silas Marner* as a wholehearted endorsement of the weaver's ultimate embrace of and by a social system from which he is at first aloof, an embrace arranged by his investment in his stepdaughter, my account means to suggest a more ambivalent reading of this tale. If the community that Silas Marner finally joins furnishes possibilities of communion unavailable to the miser, it also prohibits others. Q. D. Leavis, "Silas Marner," in *Collected Essays*, vol. 1, *The Englishness of the Novel*, ed. G. Singh (1958; reprint, Cambridge: Cambridge University Press, 1983), 275–302.

Afterword

1. Charles Dickens, *Great Expectations* (1860; reprint, New York: Penguin Books, 1985), 257.

2. Hirschman, *The Passions and the Interests*, 53.

3. Dickens, *David Copperfield*, 950.

* Works Cited *

Adorno, Theodor W. *Prisms*. Translated by Samuel Weber and Shirley Weber. Cambridge, Mass.: MIT Press, 1981.

Althusser, Louis. "Ideology and Ideological State Apparatuses (Notes Towards an Investigation)." In *Lenin and Philosophy and Other Essays*. Translated by Ben Brewster. New York: Monthly Review Press, 1971.

Armstrong, Nancy. *Desire and Domestic Fiction: A Political History of the Novel*. New York: Oxford University Press, 1987.

Attiyah, P. S. *The Rise and Fall of Freedom of Contract*. New York: Oxford University Press, 1979.

Barrett, Michele, and Mary McIntosh. *The Anti-Social Family*. New York: Verso, 1982, 1991.

Barthes, Roland. *S/Z*. Translated by Richard Miller. New York: Hill & Wang, 1974.

Basch, Françoise. *Relative Creatures: Victorian Women in Society and the Novel*. Translated by Anthony Rudolf. New York: Schocken Books, 1974.

Bataille, Georges. "The Notion of Expenditure." In *Visions of Excess: Selected Writings, 1927–1939*. Translated by Allan Stoekl. Minneapolis: University of Minnesota Press, 1985.

Baudrillard, Jean. *Critique of the Political Economy of the Sign*. Saint Louis: Telos Press, 1979.

Beer, Gillian. *Darwin's Plots: Evolutionary Narrative in Darwin, George Eliot, and Nineteenth-Century Fiction* (Boston: Routledge & Kegan Paul, 1983).

Bebel, A. *Women under Socialism*. Translated by D. De Leon. New York: Schocken Books, 1971.

Benjamin, Jessica. *Bonds of Love, Psychoanalysis, Feminism, and the Problem of Domination*. New York: Random House, 1988.

Bodichon, Barbara Lee Smith. "A Brief Summary in Plain English of the Most Important Laws Concerning Women." London, 1854.

Bolt, Christine. "Race and the Victorians." In *British Imperialism in the Nineteenth Century*. Edited by C. C. Eldridge. New York: Macmillan, 1984.

Bourdieu, Pierre. *Outline of a Theory of Practice*. Translated by Richard Nice. Cambridge: Cambridge University Press, 1977.

Brantlinger, Patrick. *Rule of Darkness: British Literature and Imperialism, 1830–1914*. Ithaca: Cornell University Press, 1988.

Brewer, Anthony. *Marxist Theories of Imperialism, A Critical Survey*. London: New Left Books, 1978.

Briggs, Asa. *The Age of Improvement, 1783–1867*. London: Longmans, Green, 1959.

Brooks, Peter. *Reading for the Plot*. New York: Random House, 1984.

Bulwer-Lytton, Edward George Earle Lytton, Baron. *England and the English*. New York: J. & J. Harper, 1833.

Butler, Judith. *Gender Trouble*. New York: Routledge, 1990.

Carlyle, Thomas. *Chartism*. London: J. Fraser, 1840.

———. *Past and Present*. Edited by Edwin Nims. 1843. New York: Charles Scribner's Sons, 1918.

Cockshut, A.O.J. *The Imagination of Charles Dickens*. New York: Random House, 1962.

Corber, Robert J. "Representing the 'Unspeakable': William Godwin and the Politics of Homophobia." *Journal of the History of Sexuality* 1, no. 1 (1990): 85–101.

Cottom, Daniel. *Social Figures: George Eliot, Social History, and Literary Representation*. Minneapolis: University of Minnesota Press, 1987.

Coward, Rosalind. *Patriarchal Precedents*. London: Routledge & Kegan Paul, 1983.

Crompton, Louis. *Byron and Greek Love: Homophobia in Nineteenth-Century England*. Berkeley: University of California Press, 1985.

Dabney, Ross H. *Love and Property in the Novels of Dickens*. Berkeley: University of California Press, 1967.

Davidoff, Leonore, and Catherine Hall, *Family Fortunes: Men and Women of the English Middle Class, 1780–1850*. London: Hutchinson, 1987.

Dickens, Charles. *Bleak House*. 1853. Reprint. London: Oxford University Press, 1951.

———. *David Copperfield*. 1850. Reprint. New York: Penguin Books, 1985.

———. *Dombey and Son*. 1848. Reprint. New York: Penguin Books, 1984.

———. *Great Expectations*. 1860. Reprint. New York: Penguin Books, 1985.

———. *Household Words*. London: Bradbury and Evans, 1850–1859.

———. *Little Dorrit*. 1857. Reprint. New York: Oxford University Press, 1982.

———. *The Mystery of Edwin Drood*. 1870. Reprint. London: Oxford University Press, 1972.

———. *Our Mutual Friend*. 1865. Reprint. New York: Penguin Books, 1985.

———. *Selected Letters*. Oxford: Oxford University Press, 1966.

Dobb, Maurice. *Theories of Value and Distribution since Adam Smith*. Cambridge and New York: Cambridge University Press, 1973.

Donzelot, Jacques. *The Policing of Families*. Translated by Robert Hurley. New York: Random House, 1979.

Eagleton, Terry. *Criticism and Ideology*. New York: New Left Books, 1976.

Eisenstein, Zillah, ed. *Capitalist Patriarchy and the Case for Socialist Feminism*. New York: Monthly Review Press, 1979.

Eldridge, C. C. *England's Mission: The Imperial Idea in the Age of Gladstone and Disraeli, 1868–80*. London: Macmillan, 1973.

———. *Victorian Imperialism*. London: Macmillan 1978.

Eliot, George. *Adam Bede*. 1859. New York: Penguin Books, 1982.

———. *Daniel Deronda*. 1876. Reprint. New York: Penguin Books, 1988.

———. *Middlemarch*. 1872. Reprint. New York: Oxford University Press, 1988.

———. *The Mill on the Floss*. 1860. Reprint. New York: Penguin Books, 1980.

———. *Silas Marner*. 1861. Reprint. New York: Penguin Books, 1985.

Eliot, T. S. "The Metaphysical Poets." In *The Sacred Wood*. London: Faber & Faber, 1920.

Ellis, Sarah. *The Wives of England, Their Relative Duties, Domestic Influence, and Social Obligations*. 1843.

———. *The Women of England*. 1839.

Engel, Monroe. *The Maturity of Dickens*. Cambridge, Mass.: Harvard University Press, 1959.

Engels, F. *The Origin of the Family, Private Property and the State*. London: Lawrence & Wishart, 1972.

Feltes, Normon. *Modes of Production of Victorian Novels*. Toronto: University of Toronto Press, 1988.

Fieldhouse, D. K. *Economics and Empire*. New York: Macmillan, 1974.

Foucault, Michel. *Discipline and Punish*. Translated by Alan Sheridan. New York: Random House, 1979.

———. *The History of Sexuality*. Vol. 1, *An Introduction*. Translated by Robert Hurley. New York: Vintage Books, 1980.

Fox-Genovese, Elizabeth, and Eugene Genovese. *Fruits of Merchant Capital*. New York: Oxford University Press, 1985.

Friedman, W. B. "Changes in Property Relations." *Transactions of the Third World Congress of Sociology* 1–2 (1956).

Fuss, Diana. *Essentially Speaking*. New York: Routledge, 1989.

Gallagher, Catherine. "The Bio-Economics of *Our Mutual Friend*." Part 3 of *Fragments of a History of the Human Body*. New York: Zone Books, 1989.

———. "George Eliot and *Daniel Deronda*: The Prostitute and the Jewish Question." In *Sex, Politics and Science in the Nineteenth-Century Novel: Selected Papers from the English Institute, 1983–1984*. Edited by Ruth Bernard Yeazell. Baltimore: Johns Hopkins University Press, 1986.

Goldman, Emma. *The Traffic in Women and Other Essays on Feminism*. New York: Times Change Press, 1971.

Habermas, Jürgen. *The Structural Transformation of the Public Sphere: An Inquiry into a Category of Bourgeois Society*. Translated by Thomas Burger. 1962. Reprint. Cambridge, Mass.: MIT Press, 1989.

Hansen, Karen V., and Ilene J. Philipson, eds. *Women, Class and the Feminist Imagination: A Socialist-Feminist Reader*. Philadelphia: Temple University Press, 1990.

Hardy, Barbara. *Particularities: Readings in George Eliot*. London: Peter Owen Press, 1982.

Harvey, A. D. "Prosecutions for Sodomy in England at the Beginning of the Nineteenth Century," *Historical Journal* 21 (1978): 939–48.

Hegel, George. *Philosophy of Right*. Translated by T. M. Knox. New York: Oxford University Press, 1967.

Helsinger, Elizabeth K., Robin Lauterbach Sheets, and William Veeder. *The Woman Question: Society and Literature in Britain and America, 1837–1883*, 3 vols. New York: Garland Publishing, 1983.

Hertz, Neil. "Some Words in George Eliot: Nullify, Neutral, Numb, Number." In *Languages of the Unsayable: The Play of Negativity in Literature and Literary Theory*. Edited by Sanford Budick and Wolfgang Iser. New York: Columbia University Press, 1989.

Hirschman, Albert O. *The Passions and the Interests: Political Arguments for Capitalism Before Its Triumph*. Princeton: Princeton University Press, 1977.

Hirst, Paul. *On Law and Ideology*. London: Macmillan, 1979.

Hobsbawm, E. J. *The Age of Capital: 1848–1875*. New York: New American Library, 1975, 1979.

Houghton, Walter E. *The Victorian Frame of Mind*. New Haven: Yale University Press, 1957.

James, Henry. *Portrait of a Lady*. 1881. Reprint. New York: Penguin Books, 1984.

Jameson, Frederic. *The Political Unconscious*. Ithaca: Cornell University Press, 1981.

Jay, Elizabeth, and Richard Jay, eds. *Critics of Capitalism*. New York: Cambridge University Press, 1986.

Kent, Susan Kingsley. *Sex and Suffrage in Britain, 1860–1914*. Princeton: Princeton University Press, 1987.

Lane, Edward William. *The Arabian Nights' Entertainments*. London: Bradbury & Evans, 1838.

Lasch, Christopher. *Haven in a Heartless World: The Family Besieged*. New York: Basic Books, 1977.

Leavis, F. R., and Q. D. Leavis. *Dickens the Novelist*. Edinburgh: R. & R. Clark, 1970.

Leavis, Q. D. *Collected Essays*. Vol. 1, *The Englishness of the Novel*. Edited by G. Singh. 1958. Reprint. Cambridge: Cambridge University Press, 1983.

Levinson, Sanford, ed. *Interpreting Law and Literature*. Evanston: Northwestern University Press, 1988.

Lévi-Strauss, Claude. "Introduction a l'oeuvre de Marcel Mauss." In *Sociologie et Anthropologie*. Paris: PUF, 1950.

Lukács, Georg. *History and Class Consciousness: Studies in Marxist Dialectics*. Translated by Rodney Livingstone. Cambridge, Mass.: MIT Press, 1971.

Lucas, John. *The Melancholy Man*. Totowa, N.J.: Harvester Press, 1980.

Macpherson, C. B. *Property: Mainstream and Critical Positions*. Toronto: Toronto University Press, 1978.

Macpherson, C. B. *The Political Theory of Possessive Individualism.* New York: Clarendon Press, 1964.

Marcus, Steven. *Dickens from Pickwick to Dombey.* New York: W. W. Norton, 1965.

Marx, Karl. *Capital.* Vol. 1. Translated by Ben Fowkes. New York: Vintage Books, 1977.

———. "The Communist Manifesto." In *Collected Works.* Vol. 6. New York: International Publishers, 1970.

———. *Early Writings.* Translated by T. B. Bottomore. New York: McGraw-Hill, 1963.

———. "Introduction to a Critique of Political Economy." In *The German Ideology.* Edited by C. J. Arthur. New York: International Publishers, 1979.

Mauss, Marcel. *The Gift: Forms and Functions of Exchange in Archaic Societies.* Translated by Ian Cunnison. New York: W. W. Norton, 1967.

Michaels, Walter Benn. *The Gold Standard and the Logic of Naturalism.* Berkeley: University of California Press, 1987.

Mill, John Stuart. *Principles of Political Economy.* Edited by Donald Winch. 1848. Reprint. New York: Penguin Books, 1970.

———. *The Subjection of Women.* Introduction by Wendall Robert Carr. 1869. Reprint. Cambridge, Mass.: MIT Press, 1970, 1988.

Miller, D. A. *Narrative and Its Discontents.* Princeton: Princeton University Press, 1981.

———. *The Novel and the Police.* Berkeley: University of California Press, 1988.

Miller, J. Hillis. Introduction to the Penguin edition of *Bleak House.* Harmondsworth: Penguin Books, 1971.

Mitchell, Juliet. *Woman's Estate.* New York: Random House, 1973.

Mulvey, Laura. "Visual Pleasure and Narrative Cinema." *Screen* 16, no. 3 (Autumn 1975): 6–18.

Myers, William. "George Eliot: Politics and Personality." In *Literature and Politics in the Nineteenth Century.* Edited by John Lucas. London: Methuen, 1971.

Newton, Judith Lowder. *Women, Power, and Subversion: Social Strategies in British Fiction, 1778–1860.* Athens: University of Georgia Press, 1981.

Patterson, Orlando. *Slavery and Social Death.* Cambridge, Mass.: Harvard University Press, 1982.

Pocock, J.G.A. *The Machiavellian Moment: Florentine Political Thought and the Atlantic Republican Tradition.* Princeton: Princeton University Press, 1975.

Polanyi, Karl. *The Great Transformation: The Political and Economic Origins of Our Time.* Boston: Beacon Press, 1944.

Poovey, Mary. *Uneven Developments: The Ideological Work of Gender in Mid-Victorian England.* Chicago: University of Chicago Press, 1988.

Pratt, Mary Louise. "Scratches on the Face of the Country; or, What Mr. Barrow Saw in the Land of the Bushmen." *Critical Inquiry* (Autumn 1985).

Reiter, Rayna, ed. *Towards an Anthropology of Women.* New York: Monthly Review Press, 1975.

Richards, Thomas. *The Commodity Culture of Victorian England.* Stanford: Stanford University Press, 1990.

Rimmon-Kenan, Shlomith. *Narrative Fiction: Contemporary Poetics.* New York: Methuen, 1983.

Rousseau, Jean-Jacques. *Discourse on the Origin and Foundation of Inequality.* Edited and translated by Roger D. Masters and Judith R. Masters. New York: St. Martin's Press, 1975.

Rowbotham, Sheila. *Woman's Consciousness, Man's World.* New York: Penguin Books, 1973.

Ruskin, John. *Sesame and Lilies.* In *Works* 18 (1923).

Ryan, Alan. *Property.* Minneapolis: University of Minnesota, 1987.

————. *Property and Political Theory.* New York: Basil Blackwell, 1984.

Ryan, Mary P. *Women in Public: Between Banners and Ballots, 1825–1880.* Baltimore: Johns Hopkins University Press, 1990.

Said, Edward. *Orientalism.* New York: Random House, 1978.

Sargeant, Lydia, ed. *Women and Revolution: A Discussion of the Unhappy Marriage of Marxism and Feminism.* Boston: South End Press, 1981.

Scarry, Elaine. *The Body in Pain.* New York: Oxford University Press, 1985.

Sedgwick, Eve Kosofsky. *Between Men: English Literature and Male Homosocial Desire.* New York: Columbia University Press, 1985.

————. *The Epistemology of the Closet.* Berkeley: University of California Press, 1990.

Shanley, Mary Lyndon. *Feminism, Marriage, and the Law in Victorian England, 1850–1895.* Princeton: Princeton University Press, 1989.

Simmel, Georg. *The Philosophy of Money.* Translated by Tom Bottomore and David Frisby. Boston: Routledge & Kegan Paul, 1978.

Sohn-Rethel, Alfred. *Intellectual and Manual Labour: A Critique of Epistemology.* Translated by Martin Sohn-Rethel. London: Macmillan Press, 1978.

Smith, Grahame. *Dickens, Money and Society.* Berkeley: University of California Press, 1968.

Stone, Lawrence. *An Open Elite?* New York: Oxford University Press, 1986.

Tawney, R. H. *The Acquisitive Society.* London: Harvester Press, 1921.

Thackeray, William Makepeace. *Vanity Fair.* 1847–48. Reprint. New York: Oxford University Press, 1983.

Thomas, Deborah. *Dickens and the Short Story.* Philadelphia: University of Pennsylvania Press, 1982.

Thompson, William. *Appeal of One Half of the Human Race, Women, against the Pretensions of the Other Half, Men, to Retain Them in Political, and Thence in Civil and Domestic Slavery.* Edited by Richard Pankhurst. 1825. Reprint. New York: Virago Press, 1983.

Thomson, David. *England in the Nineteenth Century, 1815–1914.* New York: Penguin Books, 1950, 1978.

Unger, Roberto Mangabeira. *The Critical Legal Studies Movement.* Cambridge, Mass.: Harvard University Press, 1983.

Veblin, Thorsten. *The Theory of the Leisure Class.* New York: Macmillan, 1953.

Vicinus, Martha, ed. *A Widening Sphere: Changing Roles of Victorian Women.* Bloomington: Indiana University Press, 1977.

Vogel, Lisa. "The Contested Domain: A Note on the Family in the Transition to Capitalism." *Marxist Perpectives* 1 (Spring 1978).

Wallerstein, Immanuel. *Historical Capitalism.* London: Verso, 1983.

Watt, Ian. *The Rise of the Novel.* Berkeley: University of California Press, 1957.

Weber, Max. *The Protestant Ethic and the Spirit of Capitalism.* Translated by Talcott Parsons. New York: Charles Scribner's Sons, 1958.

Weeks, Jeffrey. *Coming Out: Homosexual Politics in Britain, from the Nineteenth Century to the Present.* New York: Quartet Books, 1979.

Weiner, Annette B. *Inalienable Possessions: The Paradox of Keeping while Giving.* Berkeley: University of California Press, 1992.

Weiss, Barbara. "Secret Pockets and Secret Breasts: *Little Dorrit* and the Commercial Scandals of the Fifties." *Dickens Studies Annual* 10 (1982): 67–76.

Welsh, Alexander. *The City of Dickens.* Oxford: Clarendon Press, 1971.

———. *From Copyright to Copperfield.* Cambridge, Mass.: Harvard University Press, 1987.

Wicke, Jennifer. *Advertising Fictions: Literature, Advertisement, Social Reading.* New York: Columbia University Press, 1988.

Williams, Raymond. *The Country and the City.* New York: Oxford University Press, 1973.

Woolf, Virginia. *Three Guineas.* London: Chatto & Windus, 1938.

✳ *Index* ✳

150